# NEW DIRECTIONS FROM THE TEN COMMANDMENTS

# New Directions From The Ten Commandments

ARTHUR FAY SUELTZ

*HARPER & ROW, PUBLISHERS*
*New York, Hagerstown, San Francisco, London*

*Designed by Stephanie Krasnow*

Library of Congress Cataloging in Publication Data

Sueltz, Arthur Fay.
    New directions from the Ten Commandments.
    1. Commandments, Ten. I. Title.
BV4655.S77 1976      222'.16'066      75-36744
ISBN 0-06-067760-0

79 80 10 9 8 7 6 5 4 3

# CONTENTS

*Questions for Reflection and Discussion
are found at the end of each chapter.*

# PREFACE

This story comes from the heart of China. In a small church in a remote village the people came to the minister complaining that the wife of a deacon was stealing chickens from her neighbor. And they said, "You've got to do something about it."

He said, "All right, I will." That Sunday he preached on the text "You shall not steal." At the close of the service the deacon came to him and said, "Excellent sermon pastor."

But in three or four days the people came and said, "That sermon didn't do any good at all: she's still stealing." So the next Sunday, the minister got more specific. He said, "You shall not steal your neighbor's goods." At the close of the service the deacon shook hands and said, "That's a much better sermon. You've really got to speak specifically."

However during the week the people said, "That didn't do any good; they're still stealing." So the minister took courage in both hands and said, "You shall not steal your neighbor's chickens." The deacon came to him and said, "Now look, you're not supposed to be all that specific in the pulpit."

Yet today along with many others I find myself looking for some specific guidelines. Where can we find the moral courage and a true sense of spiritual values to get us through the "trying twenties" and "forlorn forties." Some of us come to moments when it feels like we're tearing apart the life we worked so hard to put together.

Things ought to be different. But how can we get our hands on it? "Kids ask different questions now," says Lawrence Fuchs, chairman of the American Studies Department at Brandeis University. Part of the change, says Fuchs, is the search for roots.

People have unlimited choices at exactly the time when a value system within which to make such choices seems in doubt. A lot of us long for a new spirit. Something we can sink our roots into. Must the unraveling of modern society be followed by the making of a new social order, even new gods?

If old dogmas have lost their power to terrify, have all the older values lost their power to inspire? If they have, why today do so many long to get in touch again with their origins? It feels like a light has begun to dawn in the minds of men everywhere. Something similar to the light that dawned after the "dark ages." No one can remain indifferent in the face of such an upheaval.

When we start talking values and origins, I believe we're talking God. But when I look around and see what goes on in this world, it sometimes looks like God has moved on to greener pastures. Yet I live in a world where everything's on the move. Nothing stays still. People move all over the country and the world. And people move in their perceptions and understandings. Everybody and everything is on the move. Suppose God's no exception to that! Suppose God is not "the great exception" to everything else we know and see and touch. Suppose everything that happens, happens also to God. Can such a God give us any guidelines that will help us sink our roots down into the movement of spiritual reality? I believe he can, and does. Will such guidelines help us cope with the physical and psychological overload of today and develop fresh ways of thinking and living together in peace? I believe so.

Centuries ago another people on the move were asked to take ten words as navigational aids for their personal and national life. Ten buoys marked out the channel and warned them where dangerous rocks and shoals lay hidden. These people took Ten Commandments from God as seriously as a navigator takes any aid to navigation. They wanted to stay in the channel of creative living. Yes, economic, political, and social sickness affect the quality of life on this planet. But behind them all lurks a furtive divided spiritual allegiance.

Though each chapter in this book uses one of the Ten Commandments as a guideline, the book is not just an exposition of the Ten Commandments. Rather I hope to rediscover with you some specific directions that will lead us to fuller lives as persons and as a society.

The passages I quote from the Bible usually follow the Revised Standard Version or the New English Bible. But I often paraphrase rather than quote word-for-word.

So many people have helped me in my pilgrimage. I've soaked up their ideas and insights like a sponge. I've tried to give credit wherever I could. But I'm sure some ideas expressed here as my own have their roots in the minds and hearts of others who have contributed so much to my life.

ARTHUR FAY SUELTZ

*Long Beach, California*

# INTRODUCTION:
# A QUEST FOR ROOTS

A lot of us who work hard and pay our taxes don't sleep well at night. We argue about everything and agree on nothing. Why doesn't life work? In the darkness, I get to wondering: "Art, what can you do about anything anyway. Maybe your friend was right in saying that God has either gone mad or is just a damn fool."

My spirits sink—which reminds me that I have them. For a long time I shied away from questions of the spirit. Suddenly they seem important. A whole dimension of life I'd half forgotten resurfaced. I say half forgotten because every time I'd hear, "he gave a spirited talk," or "she's a spirited girl," I sensed some such dimension existed.

So with many others, I started on a quest for spiritual roots. I remembered an old story of a college professor named A². A² lived in Flat Land. Everything in Flat Land had just two dimensions, height and breadth. Nothing had depth. If a friend turned sideways, you couldn't see him. People lived in flat houses, ate flat meals, drank flat cokes, thought flat thoughts, and lived flat lives.

A² taught higher mathematics at the university. One night, he threw a party for some of his friends. Upstairs his precocious little son, Pentagon, tried to sleep. As he tossed on his bed, he began to dream. He dreamed a dream no one had dreamed before. Suddenly, Pentagon dreamed that everything had not only height and breadth, but depth! Houses and trees and especially girls looked so different. He felt different. Life took on a whole new scope. This new dimen-

sion affected the way people thought and acted. Then, as
unexpectedly as it had started, the dream ended.

Pentagon couldn't keep a dream like that locked up inside
himself. His bare feet hit the floor and carried him downstairs
right into the middle of his father's party. There he stood in
his rumpled pajamas pouring out a dream of an unheard-of
dimension of life. Pentagon tried to explain what depth
looked like and felt like. People didn't have to go on living
flat little lives and thinking flat little thoughts. They could
sink their roots down into a whole new dimension of depth.

$A^2$ couldn't hide his embarrassment. Nor could he shut
Pentagon up. The party ended in a shambles. Far into the
night, $A^2$ tried to reason with his son. But Pentagon stamped
his foot and kept saying that another dimension of life existed.

The next morning, Pentagon talked to anybody who would
listen. People thought the poor boy had lost touch with reality. So for the sake of his sanity and theirs, they locked him
up. But now, $A^2$ didn't sleep well at night. Perhaps things
could be different. Maybe they ought to be.

Life today has a strange one-dimensional quality. No
depth of the past and no sharp awareness of the future—just
the dimension of the present. As though the world began
last Saturday night.

Recently, many people have come to feel the need for a
new depth of spiritual reality. In this quest, new currents
carry people off in different directions. A few years ago saw
the rise of a renewed interest in Eastern religions. Then
came a boom in astrology. And today ordinary people out in
the suburbs practice witchcraft and dabble in devil worship.
In the meantime, many churches look like ships becalmed
with sails flapping, not a breath of wind anywhere.

Frankly, a lot of people simply do not believe in God any-
more. Perhaps more than I'd like to admit. Many of these
people won't deny God's existence. They simply feel that life
does not offer convincing evidence of his presence in the
world.

Others say, "God may exist, but so what? His existence or

his nonexistence makes no difference to me. I believe the pyramids exist in Egypt, but I've never been there. I've never seen them. And frankly, whether the pyramids exist or not has little effect on how I live. If they disappeared tomorrow, it wouldn't affect my life. OK God exists, but so what." God's existence or nonexistence does not affect them.

That of course is an extreme example. Yet all my life, I've run into people who say they believe in God but practically speaking order their lives as though God did not exist.

But now even that mood has changed. Fewer people than ever feel compelled to give God lip service. It's easy and popular to say you've stopped believing in God. It sounds liberated. Many of the "best people"—intellectuals, philosophers, scientists, artists, politicians—say they don't believe. So in spite of a widespread spiritual hunger, churches today can no longer coast along assured of broad popular support. Nothing disastrous about that. In fact, it may get some of us church members to grapple with basic realities.

In fact I'm beginning to sense a widespread quest for spiritual depth inside the Church as well as outside it. Why should Christians feel compelled to compete with each other as if they were enemies instead of brothers? Why should they feel like aliens and strangers instead of partners? A lot of us inside the Church feel the need of a new spirit. Iris Murdock describes the mood as "a new humility which favors clarity and plain speech, the expression of obvious unpretentious truth by returning to the deep and obvious and ordinary things of human existence and making there a place for cool speech and wit and serious unforced reflection." [1]

But today, the foundations of culture shake beneath my feet. I'm torn with doubt about the reliability of values I used to take for granted. Violence at home and abroad make the shallow little dreams of church-going people living by the Golden Rule look ridiculous. I need a more realistic understanding and experience of God than that. I need some-

1. James I. McCord, *Princeton Alumni News*, 1972, p. 1.

thing more than an ornament or a prop to an otherwise ade-
quate life.

Other men have had similar experiences. In the Bible,
they wrote down what they had come to believe, out of such
experiences. They sensed the power of God loose in creation.
They also sensed the Spirit of God loose in their history.

These men lived as slaves in Egypt. They made bricks
without enough straw to do a good job. Slaves came cheap.
If you didn't obey the simplest order, you died. If you reported in sick, no one treated you—you died. Yet they said
a living God had selected them as the people through whom
he would show the power of his love and justice to all the
world. They believed God began that process by choosing
Moses to lead them on the greatest freedom march the world
had yet seen. "I am the Lord your God," they said they heard
him say, "who brought you out of the land of Egypt, out of
the house of bondage. I did that."

If they're right, there's a God loose in the world who cares
about how I vote and how I spend my money, and what the
president decides, and whether or not a workingman's income
keeps pace with corporate profits. Yes, he lets me play the
game. He lets me make stupid moves and take ridiculous
risks. But he keeps the lead in his hand, and in the end
calls the plays.

But Moses found himself involved with people having a
hard time coping with a physical, psychological, and spiritual
overload. Somehow they had to put their lives and their
society together. Where should they start? In the desert near
Mount Sinai something happened. Out of a profound experience of God came ten words for the humanizing of their
life together. Liberating words. Ten commandments. Not exactly the kind of word any of them expected. People often
don't give a hoot whether or not God's word ever gets spoken.
A book about the Ten Commandments? Hardly what the
world is waiting for! But did the world ever give a damn
about them?

And even in church how many today feel we have outgrown the Ten Commandments? Sometimes it feels like we middle-class church members have remade our churches in our own image. Harry Golden commented in a recent speech:

As the middle-class proliferated, their need for self-expression also grew. Lacking the talent or inclination for politics, the traditional province for the rich man's personal ambition, the well-off layman found he could fulfill his hunger for expression by managing his church.

He along with others like him gave the church money, and then they formed a church committee and decided jointly how they would spend it. Eventually, too, this committee began to oversee the content of the Sunday sermon, since they wanted their church to reflect them, not their minister, who was now but an agent.

So our sense of moral judgment and spiritual muscle began to wither away. Thousands of Americans today find nothing wrong in stealing anything, from hotel ashtrays to the private files of psychiatrists and the vaults of public confidence. Rip-off has become a social staple.

And what can you call the soaring profits of some huge corporation in the face of scarcities but rip-off?

So what happened to our sense of what's important? Has it disappeared? Have we banished it to some other planet? Now, if ever, a lot of us, ranging from white collar to hard hat to blue jeans, need to sink our roots down deeply into that basic dimension of reality. How to recognize beauty and reject ugliness. How to stand up to brutality committed against us by unresponsive government—local, state, and federal. If we can rediscover how to do some of these things a rebirth of values may follow. Clearly we stand in critical need of just such a common and individual rebirth. The sooner the better. Lest our battered society break up on the rocks of chaos and moral emptiness.

So when it comes to a sense of what's important I feel a pinching scarcity. For instance, Vince Lombardi once said, "Winning isn't important—winning is everything." Maybe that's OK for football. After all football isn't all that important. But when it comes to real life affairs such as

Watergate and the events related to it, suddenly Lombardi's dictum "Winning isn't important—winning is everything" becomes lethal to our political survival as a free society. All at once I face the criminalization of politics. Can we let politicians explain their criminal acts on the grounds that what they did was good for America and would save their political party from disgrace?

Somehow I can't just sit back and sigh, "Dear God, what a mess!" Suddenly I sense there's more to religion than giving assent to an ancient creed, betting a buck a week God exists, attending worship now and then, saying an occasional prayer when in trouble, and generally reflecting the religious ideas of my society. God's commands do not simply echo the quaint conventions of a passing culture. I believe through them he has word for me today. And I believe a great reservoir of good will still exists in people. A growing number have begun to care about such things as integrity, compassion, honesty, and faith.

The world needs all the life it can get right now. But I believe it needs *new* life! A new spirit. Man remains the big question mark in everything. Everything will depend on what kind of changes takes place in men. I believe the only real good and lasting change occurs in a man's spirit. None of us can get rid of all the evil on earth. Few of us can turn things around in this world even a little bit. But what if I could make this questionable world just a little more just, a little more free, a little more satisfying. Who knows what might happen if a few of us in this rapidly deteriorating civilization began to rise out of the defensiveness that makes us bristle when someone irritates or criticizes us, to rise out of our hunger for power and privilege and profit. If I could just begin to rise and affirm the beauty of decency, the joy of generosity, the indispensability of integrity. If I could rise to the point where I could see the futility of making more money than I need, of chasing pleasures that evaporate as quickly as the morning dew. Only God knows what might happen if a few of us let ourselves go to do the thing that lies closest to us, what we know Jesus would do if he stood where we stood!

So in my quest, I discover a God deeply involved in the whole history of mankind. What a liberating discovery! It lets me see justice as more than man-made house rules or organizational bylaws. It helps me recover my sense of accountability.

I used to play golf quite a bit. I enjoyed it. But as Ernest Campbell suggests in *No-Fault Morality* the game has a way of getting the best of me. When I started out, I played with some very generous fellows. If on the first tee I hopelessly shanked the shot, they'd say, "Art, we won't count it. We'll call it a 'mulligan.' Hit it again." In grateful desperation, I'd hit it again. And then I discovered that this mutual grace knew no bounds when we got to the green. Picture the scene: a man's ball lies fifteen feet from the cup. He says to his friend, "I'll give you yours if you'll give me mine." They look over their shoulders to see if heaven is watching, and then say, "Deal."

And so, I have an idea that all over America, thousands of guys take "mulligans" on the first tee and others, and "gimmees" on every other hole, and think they're playing golf! They decide by mutual consent as they go along which strokes they'll count and which strokes they won't count. But such mutual consent raises a question: where does par come in? Who speaks for par? And when anyone raises that question, I suddenly sense the presence of a third element. Whenever I play golf with a friend, I have to ask myself, "Do he and I really have complete liberty to determine which strokes we'll count and which strokes we won't count?"

When it comes to right and wrong in world affairs, can we by mutual consent determine that the role of the United States is beyond question? Can we domesticate justice like that? Or, more personally, does mutual consent in sexual perversity make the act right? Or am I accountable to someone higher than mutual consent? I believe I am.

I've read a lot of articles about the rise in popularity of

Jesus, especially among some of our younger people. That's great! But I wonder whether or not the "Jesus movement" has turned out to be the real thing. It looks so "superspiritual." And I remember how William Temple once cautioned that the word "spiritual" can be the most dangerous word in the Christian vocabulary. Dangerous because it can mean little more than a kind of vague, tranquilized unconcern for anything except the next world.

In striking contrast to that, the men who wrote the Bible repeatedly talked about how God did things in their material and secular world. None of them talked about Someone vague and otherworldly. They talked about Someone who affected their lives in specific ways that turned the world upside down. They could not work his Spirit up nor could they manipulate or control him. He went way beyond their organized religion. And they saw God's Spirit impressively incarnate in Jesus. It's his Spirit that gives life when the letter kills.

Yet being impressed with the Spirit of God loose in Jesus is one thing. Being impressed with Jesus may get some people started on the road to faith. But Jesus never wanted admirers. He kept looking for followers. If I met him in the flesh, would I ask him for orders or for his autograph? That's the question.

In my quest, I discover a God who cares about the total life of people. I'm accountable to him. He cares how my life comes out. He's not so much a God of positive thinking or possibility thinking, who's always on my side, doing what I want him to do when I need him to do it and making things come out right for me. Rather, out of his concern that we not make shipwreck of our lives or of our society, God has given us ten clear warnings of rocky shores and dangerous shoals.

Furthermore, in Jesus I begin to see that kind of truth translated into flesh and blood. Because he lived what he spoke, his work has the kind of authority I'm looking for. He never talked about faith in God and then went out and lived scared to death of everything, as I do. That's the kind of reality I'd like to base my life on.

## QUESTIONS FOR REFLECTION AND DISCUSSION

1. Have you ever felt that God is an underachiever in this world?
2. Do you think middle-class Christians have remade the church in their own image?
3. How do you feel about Vince Lombardi's statement: "Winning isn't important—winning is everything"?
4. If you met Jesus in the flesh, would you ask for guidance or for his autograph?

# 1. EXCLUSIVELY YOURS

> You shall have no other gods before me.
> *Exodus 20:3*

In the movie *Save the Tiger,* Jack Lemmon won an Academy Award for playing the part of a man produced by the world of the 1940 Brooklyn Dodgers and World War II. Harry accepted as good and bad pretty much what his parents did, and their parents before them. Now he feels lost. "There are no rules anymore, just referees." Everything's relative. But relative to what?

Whenever I start talking about why I value what I value I find I'm talking God, regardless of what words I use.

In trying to sink my roots down into the stream of reality, I suddenly strike something hard. I sense someone saying, "You shall have no other gods."

The people who first heard that lived in a world with as many gods as there were countries. Isis of Egypt, Moloch and Baal of Canaan. If they crossed the border they came under the jurisdiction of another god. Suddenly they hear that wherever they go just one God matters. And no place, no culture, no time, no other gods can shut him out.

Hearing that today something within me says, "Dear God, that sounds terribly intolerant. 'You shall have no other gods!' Much too exclusive. Unreasonable. All men don't see things that same way, especially when it comes to religion. What may be true for one man may not be true for another. Look at the great religions of the world like Hinduism and Buddhism. The broad-minded Hindu will take Jesus Christ and the Christian God and set them right alongside all the other gods and give them equal status. God, you're far too exclusive in your claim that I should have no other gods beside you."

Yet "no other god" keeps sounding like a trumpet in my mind. Religious truth, like all other truth, has an offensive exclusiveness about it. Truth will not admit the validity of its opposite. If I claim that Sacramento is the capital of California and you say that San Francisco is, one of us is wrong! It makes no sense to say that what is true for you is not true for me. Truth stands alone.

I get direction in life not by admitting what is true for you is not true for me. I get direction by going after truth, and when I find it, following it.

So I'm discovering that when I look for truth, I'm looking for God. In this sense, all of us have a god. We either have the God who made us, or the gods we make. The question is which.

"I am the Lord your God. You shall have me—nothing else will do. You can't get rid of me. I'm your God. Exclusively. I will never leave you or forsake you." That sounds like there's a God loose who will not admit the validity of any rival. And if that's false, then it's time I found out about it and quit a lot of nonsense.

All kinds of things inside of me and outside of me want to run my life. It often feels like a hundred god's vie for my loyalty. For instance, inside of me I feel a strong urge to get ahead. But getting ahead soon clamors for all my time, my energy, my thought, and my allegiance. It urges me to spend money on things that will make me look like a winner. It urges me to get rid of friends that stand in the way of my "getting ahead." It will urge me to cheat on an insurance claim if I think I can get away with it.

Now as C. Ellis Nelson in his book *Love and the Law* suggests, if I choose to live for "getting ahead," what does it matter how many times I go to church or what church I go to! I'll simply use the church like I do everything and everybody else, to "get ahead." Because that's the god I'm living for.

So a lot of us have sensed the inadequacy of these conflicting and competing desires within us and have looked for something outside ourselves. And here again I've discovered all kinds of causes clamoring for my loyalty. Good causes. Causes with names like "world peace" or "human dignity" or "ending poverty" or "equal opportunity for women."

Now there's one! "Equal opportunity for women." Frankly, I'm very sympathetic with most of the objectives of the women's movement because I remember Jesus. Jesus lived in a male-dominated society. In his society, women had few, if any, rights. A woman's word didn't count in court. A man could divorce his wife and throw her out on the street penniless, simply because she burned his dinner. Yet Jesus, in that kind of society, dared to describe God in terms of a woman looking for a coin she'd lost in her house. Jesus talked of God in manly terms and in womanly terms as though the two of them together, somehow, best described God's nature. And yet causes, no matter how good, are at best means to an end. Unfortunately, they often become the end in themselves. And when they do, they assume the prerogatives of an absolute, a god, by which I must determine all my other values. When that happens, a cause can be little more than a disguise for getting my own way. Like the zealous young feminist who smashes her home in the name of women's liberation.

And I've seen people do much the same thing with patriotism. I love this country. My forefathers fought for its liberation. I haven't forgotten that. But I continue to meet people who tell me that loyalty to my country means doing whatever my country tells me to do. They want me to make an absolute, that is a god, out of the policy of my country. And I think some of us have moments of terrible tension right at that point. Some of us remember how both Hitler and Stalin demanded complete loyalty to the policies of the state. And we remember how almost nobody in those countries dared oppose them. We remember how the newspapers stopped printing critical editorials. We remember how the universities began to go along with the party line in Germany and in Russia. Labor unions supported government policies. But we also remember how a relatively few Christians and Jews in both countries dared oppose the absolute authority of the state. They risked their lives to do it. "What did they have?" asked Elton Trueblood. "They had the first commandment." [1]

So I find in my day as Moses found in his a world full of national gods. Each country treating its policy as an absolute.

This old commandment helps me in times of such confused national values. It helps me see that loyalty to the truth is the greatest loyalty I can give my country. It frees me to correct a friend's behavior when it violates simple justice. Simply to overlook injustice distorts the meaning of friendship. After setting right the church at Galatia Paul asks: "Have I now become your enemy by telling the truth?" I'd be disloyal to my country to do anything less than speak and live as much of the truth as I know. Criticism remains a vital part of a free society. Without it men bring on themselves some sort of totalitarian control. Patriotism means commitment to truth and justice and self-sacrifice.

Then for a while some of us looked to technology to give us the truth. After all, we'd seen disease after disease go down before the onslaught of modern technology. Polio, humbled by the Salk vaccine. We may now stand on the edge of a breakthrough on cancer. And suddenly before I know it, science turns into scientism—an attempt to make one method of understanding truth about the physical world the only way to know any truth. As though we just needed a few more years, a few more technologists, a few more economists, a few more sociologists, a few more statistics, and we can save ourselves! And yet technology remains a tool. Hasn't our trouble always come down to what we've done to each other with our tools?

And still a whole lot of people just take life as it comes and go on working and living for as much money as they

1. Elton Trueblood, *Foundations for Reconstruction* (New York: Harper & Bros., 1946), p. 14.

can get. I've watched people sacrifice their health and their families on that altar. Paul saw the same thing in his day. He put those who serve this particular god in the same bag with those who practiced prostitution. He felt they went to-gether. Times have changed since then, especially in coun-tries where we derive so many of our values from the profit motive. Clarence Jordan once suggested that we don't kick a man who lets money making be the controling factor in his life out of the Church. We tend to make him a member of some committee, or a deacon or an elder—especially if he tithes!

So all kinds of gods clamor for the control of my life. I feel pulled first in one direction and then in another. Yet as I penetrate deeper into the stream of spiritual reality, none of them seem big enough to satisfy my hunger for living. I keep hearing someone saying, "Art, you must have me. If you could take the whole world and get it inside of your soul, it would rattle around like a dry bean. You can't squeeze more out of the world than there is in it. I've made you for some-thing bigger. I've made you for myself. Furthermore, you can only have one god at a time. I am exclusively yours. You can't serve God and country, or God and money, or God and anything else on equal terms. You shall have no other god besides me. If you're serious about that, you'll have to let the others go."

Suddenly the dimension of God's exclusiveness hits me full force. I'm a preacher. If God's really God of the Church, then I can't use the pulpit as a platform from which I can prattle my own prejudices. God declares himself the central authority in our congregation. That makes the Church his rather than ours. And as that comes back into focus, I see that what matters in church is not the will of the pastor, or the will of the church officers, or the will of the congregation, but the will of God! Strange how that has a way of slipping out of focus.

Bob McNeil, in his book *God Wills Us Free*, tells of a church officer caught in a heated emotional debate at a board meeting of his church in Alabama. The officers argued with

each other about the moral responsibility of that church in
that city. Someone suggested that the gospel of Christ demanded a specific action in the community. At that point,
this church officer stood and heartedly replied, "To hell with
the gospel of Jesus Christ—we've got to think of the harmony
of this church!" As though the church belonged to the church
board and to the people, to do with as they pleased.

So when someone asked Jesus which commandment took
precedence over all the others, he didn't say, "You shall not
commit adultery, or you shall not use illegal drugs, or you
should not steal, or you shouldn't lie." He said, "You shall
love the Lord your God with all your heart, and with all
your soul, and with all your mind, and with all your strength."

When those aggressive Israelites swarmed out of Egypt
they camped for a while on the borders of Balak's tiny kingdom. The worried king sent for the seer Balaam. He prom-
ised to pay him well if he would put a curse on these threatening newcomers.

A strange, complex man, Balaam. At first he refused the
king's generous offer. Somehow he felt he could not curse
whom God had blessed. He sent the king's messengers away.
But felt depressed because he hated to lose the money the
king offered.

At such times strange things go on in men's minds. Balaam
wanted to keep faith with God. He also wanted the money
the king offered. Finally he decided to go and try to curse
the Israelites. He made up his mind to speak as much of the
truth as he could. Like a man who will not tolerate dishonesty
in his associates if he knows it. It's just that he does his best
to keep from knowing it.

However when Balaam came to the crucial moment he
found he didn't have it in him to pronounce the curse. But he
did have some advice for King Balak. Advice that I think
grew out of his recent experience. He knew how the Israelites could bring ruin on themselves. "Make them believe,"
he advised the king, "that God will bless them regardless of
how they live, so long as they give him the lip service of
worship. Convince them they can marry the cultural values

of the Bedouin society that now surround them. Tell them
they can adjust the truth of God so it will fit into the ethical
values of whatever culture they find themselves in." On this
basis, as Louis Cassels once suggested, one can translate
the Ten Commandments to read:
   "Thou shalt not steal—much."
   "Thou shalt not commit adultery—except when you're really
in love."
   "Thou shalt not bear false witness—unless you're in a jam."
Honest up to a point. Truthful most of the time. No one wants
to repeal the truth of God. It's just that we don't want to
carry it too far. Sure I want to feel clean. But I also want to
keep on doing the things that make me unclean.
   Some of the values I call respectable, Jesus calls sin. When
Jesus talked about loving the Lord your God with all your
heart and all your mind and all your soul, he said it to perfectly respectable middle-class people. He pointed out how
many of them loved to look like winners. They fought for the
best seats; they simply valued their standing in the community more than they did God. He warned them about the dan-
gers of "laying up for yourselves treasures on earth." Jesus
called it a sin always to invite friends for dinner, and never
provide for the feeding of the poor. He seemed to feel that I
can't tell a dead man about God's love, and if a man dies
of starvation, he may never hear about it.
   And what about the whole idea of individualism, private
enterprise, and the profit motive in the light of God's exclusive claim on our lives? I value individual human dignity.
I value a job well done. And I know a little bit about human
motivation. Yet a lot of public and private talk about a
"work ethic" bothers me. Some hard-headed Christians called
Puritans brought with them to our shores habits of hard
work and thrift. These values greatly influenced the shape
and style of life in our country. Yet for whatever their short-
comings these founders of our society valued work not so
much for what the individual could profit from it, but for
what that hard work would contribute to the glory of God
and the welfare of the community. But today when I hear

people talking about profit they usually mean that a person motivated by an aggressive spirit should work hard to get as much as he can for himself. Profit suddenly becomes more important than people and their needs. Rugged individualism gets boiled down to a crude kind of sociological Darwinism, the survival of the fittest. And that simply is not the gospel.

Once Jesus went to work to bring a man to his senses and rid him of the spiritual divisions that tore him apart. Jesus had to get rid of a whole herd of pigs to do it. A strange story, yet the first three Gospels tell it.

Jesus came to the end of a day of preaching. He was dead tired. To get away from it all, he said to his disciples, "Let's go on over across the lake." So, they got in the boat and went across the Sea of Galilee. As they dragged the boat ashore on the other side, from somewhere out of the darkness came an angry, naked, bedeviled man. A man whom society didn't know what to do with nor how to control; neither could he control himself. So, they banished him to live in the tombs —a place of dead dreams and broken, shattered hopes. For the sake of order in the community, they put him out of their sight and out of their minds.

But he kept coming back. So they chained him to the rocks. They met force with force. But he kept breaking chains, he just didn't know what else to do. And finally, he began to use the rocks to cut and tear himself to pieces.

Now, through the shadows, he saw another gang of men coming ashore, perhaps to chain and beat him again. So, he came screaming toward them, out of the dark, with bits of chain flying from his powerful wrists and his legs.

You could almost smell the fear in the disciples as they edged back toward the boat. But Jesus stood there on the sand. Then, taking his own life in his hands, he started to walk toward this violent, dangerous man and asked, "What is your name?" He reached for the man's very self.

"My name is Legion." And with that word this man confessed that there were many selves within him vying for the mastery of his life—"*My name is Legion.*"

In a profound sense, that describes my experience. I, too, have many selves clamoring for attention, clamoring for allegiance. And I sense Jesus approaching me, asking my name in order to heal that inner division of body and soul.

Now in order to get this man back in his right mind Jesus had to deal with an economic problem in that society. With shocking disregard for private property and expected profits he healed the man and got rid of the pigs. People reacted immediately. "Jesus, get out of here! Your putting this man back in his right mind cost us our pigs. You value men—we value pigs. If you don't get out of here you'll wreck our whole economy." In order to deal with the inner divisions that destroy our humanity and sense of community, Jesus had to deal with some very real social conditions that contribute to our madness. And that's the Gospel! He simply put human wholeness, individual and corporate, above property and profit.

So from Jesus, I learn I may have to get rid of some perfectly "respectable" values if I'm serious about the exclusive nature of God. And that's not easy. I mean I could very easily exchange one set of values for another. I could easily exchange values that emphasize man's private relationship with God for another set of values that emphasizes God's concern for society and justice. If I did that, I'd face the temptation to feel more concern about racial justice than about sexual perversion. I could get so caught up in social issues that I can't overcome them—they overcome me. Suddenly I see that having "no other gods before me" means that those who tell me to keep the Church's nose out of personal issues are just as wrong as those who tell me to keep the Church's nose out of the secular and political issues. This First Commandment declares that no value system, religious or otherwise, supersedes the God who revealed himself in Christ as the point of reference for all of life.

As I begin to take that seriously, I find myself standing again in the shadow of the Cross. Jesus took God seriously, and I know what happened to him. That's the trouble. Yet

I find it terribly hard to stand there in the shadow of the Cross and look up and say, "I'm sorry about what happened to you, but honestly I have some other interests I have to take care of. I've got my reputation to look out for. And I'm not sure I could stick with you if I felt public opinion weighed heavily against what you clearly stand for. 'You shall have no other gods before me' sounds too difficult for me."

And it is. And then I remember how Jesus once said, "Come unto me; take my yoke upon you, learn of me . . ." The words "learn of me," suddenly leap right out of the text. Jesus talks as though he doesn't expect me to get there all at once. And I think back about how his first disciples lived and learned. But he does expect me to "learn of him." I believe I can learn how to behave as if I had a God who will never leave us or forsake us.

I received this letter from a friend of mine who serves in the California State Legislature.

Dear Art:

As I am sitting here at the Sacramento Airport this A.M. feeling very sorry for myself, I took out two of your recent sermons and re-read them.

I have problems, or at least they seemed problems when I arrived. To have to leave home at 8 A.M. on Father's Day to campaign in hostile and unfriendly areas for openers. Problems with legislation that I feel is for the public's interest only to be blocked by special narrow interests.

But I see now that God's world is so much larger than mine. His concern for humans makes my feeble attempts both worthwhile at the same time as I realize that His plan is much larger than I can envision. . . . This has given me the courage to face this day with unimaginable strength.

## QUESTIONS FOR REFLECTION AND DISCUSSION

1. Do you think the God of the Bible is the only god there is?
2. How do you feel about the statement: "There are no rules any-more, just referees"?

3. Can what is true for me ever not be true for you? Why? Why not?
4. Do you believe you cannot serve God and country, or God and money, or God and anything else on equal terms?
5. If you knew God would never give up on you, how would you feel?

# 2. QUESTIONS OF AUTHORITY

You shall not make for yourself a graven image, or any like-
ness of anything that is in heaven above, or that is in the
earth beneath, or that is in the water under the earth; you
shall not bow down to them or serve them; for I the Lord your
God am a jealous God, visiting the iniquity of the fathers upon
the children to the third and the fourth generation of those who
hate me, but showing steadfast love to thousands of those who
love me and keep my commandments.

*Exodus 20:4-6*

Believing God is my God raises questions of authority. During the war in Southeast Asia, the Los Angeles *Times* ran an
editorial quoting then Air Force Chief of Staff General John
D. Ryan. General Ryan told a Senate committee investigat-
ing unauthorized bombing raids against North Vietnam that
he couldn't guarantee that such incidents wouldn't happen
again. The issue highlighted the whole question of command,
control, and authority.

How often, like General Ryan, I'd rather control authority
than be controlled by it. So would the people who traveled
with Moses. But how can you relate to or control an authority you can't see? That's what "You shall not make for
yourself a graven image" is getting at.

The question of authority seems to be the most disturbing
problem of our time. Parents feel it. Judges feel it. The leaders of the Russian Communist party feel it. The Pope feels it.
Many sources of authority today have rebellions on their
hands. When people question the validity of an authority, can
that authority ever re-establish itself?

Suppose persons and institutions lose their credibility to the degree that they fail to recognize any ultimate authority. Doesn't failure to recognize any final authority leave my conscience at the mercy of my love for power, my love for money, my love for sex, or my love for status? If so, many of our young people may have rebelled not against "authority" but against "no authority."

The writer Ralph Keyes sensed this as he approached his thirtieth birthday. He wrote:

Slowly, perhaps unwillingly, but surely, I'm developing my own hangups about the "youth problem." I find it hard to be with young people more than a few years younger than myself, no matter how much our uniforms—our Levis, hair and beards—signal brotherhood. I've been beaten around and defeated by insoluble problems, as have most of my friends in their late twenties, in ways that are inexplicable to anyone much younger.

My realization that I'll never solve all my own problems, let alone the world's feels to me like the beginning of wisdom—even if younger acquaintances consider it closer to cynicism.

He admits that some of the kids in his college class seem put off by this admission—and scared of it. He comments further, "When I pressed an eighteen-year-old to explain why, she finally blurted out, 'Well, if you're so much older than we are and still haven't got it together, then what do we have to look forward to?'" [1] Is there no final authority anywhere?

A lot of people in mid-career wonder the same thing. "Why, in their mid-thirties, do so many people suddenly crack up, break down, let their careers go smash, or lash out at those closest to them?" asks Kenn Rogers.

He quotes one man in his mid-thirties as saying, "What do you want me to tell you? I wake up at three in the morning; I feel paunchy and tired. I look at my wife snoring next to

1. Kenn Rogers, "The Mid-Career Crisis," *Saturday Review of the Society,* February 1973, p. 73.

me with two pounds of make-up smeared all over her face. Both of my kids, God bless them, are inches taller than I am. Both tell me that I'm a square and a supporter of a hypocritical society. Big deal. I then think of the job, and I just know they are going to make Harry executive vice-president and not me. My secretary will be consoling, always ready to flirt. Stupid broad. You can't get involved in the office. Weekends I play golf at the country club, have a couple of drinks, go home, eat, watch TV, play cards with the neighbors, hear a little gossip, go to bed, go to work. Come next August, I'll be thirty-seven. I often wonder, 'How is this different from what my old man and my mother used to do?' Except their way of life wasn't as expensive as mine. They were never as much in hock as I am. Things aren't at all the way I thought they would be. Sometimes I think: screw it all! But I can't just run out. Christ! What the hell do I do?"

Rogers goes on to suggest that such anxious feelings grow out of the feeling that one will not live as long as one already has. No doubt. But I'm still left with the haunting question, "What do I do?" That's a question about authorization of behavior. A question of authority. Of whom do you ask such questions?

Against this background, Peter Berger called for a new stance. "It seems to me," he says, "that it is time to say enough to the dance around the golden calves of modernity." [2]

Dr. Berger does not call for a reactionary hard-line authoritarianism. A hard-line authoritarianism simply emphasizes rules regardless of their relationship to reality. Unfortunately I sense a "growing authoritarianism" among desperate people in our society. Authoritarian churches suddenly begin breaking growth records. Such movements have little trouble meeting any budget they set. Yet real moral authority differs from authoritarianism at the point of its relationship to truth.

2. Peter Berger, "A Call for Authority," *New World Outlook*, January 1972, pp. 8–9.

At this point, Dr. Berger suggests that "perhaps we Christians may have more and better than we gave ourselves
credit for." [3]

Once a fierce, militant collection of ex-slaves stood at the
foot of Mount Sinai. A restless, hot, ill-tempered, ill-organ-
ized, insecure, frustrated group. Sure, Moses got them out
from under Pharaoh's heel. But then who likes to feel in-
debted to anyone else for his manhood? That's something
I'd rather work out for myself.

Besides, Moses kept saying God had chosen them as people
through whom he wanted to show his love and justice to all
the world. But no one had seen this God Moses kept talking
about. Yes, Moses said, God provided manna for them to eat
in the desert. But it looked like the miracle came from the
secretion of insects they saw flying around. Yes, Moses said
God made water flow from a rock. But then maybe old
Moses just took his staff and pried a rock off a top of a hidden
underground spring.

Anyway Moses had gone off to the top of Mount Sinai
again to talk with his God. They hadn't seen him for almost
a month. And suddenly, everybody got fed up with the whole
deal. They'd had a bellyful of Moses and his God-talk and
his miracles. So they came to Aaron, the brother of Moses,
and said, "Make us gods that shall go before us. As for this
Moses, we don't know what's become of him."

Aaron had a rebellion on his hands. Nothing ignorant, or
unsophisticated, or irreligious about it either. These people
simply wanted a reasonable authority for their lives. They
wanted an authority cut down to a manageable size. After
all, who wants an authority forever making huge demands
on my time, my thought, my energy, my behavior, and always poking holes in my favorite ideas and assumptions?
I'd much rather have an authority that lets me alone until
I want him. An authority that likes what I like, and hates
what I hate. An authority who depends on me to protect him
against the sinister onslaughts of all those who conspire

3. Berger, *Ibid.*

against him. An authority who owes me something for that protection. And if this god will not make his will for my life clear and painless and fun, I'll simply leave him behind.

So these people brought their gold and melted it down and made a golden calf. They still wanted a god, but they wanted a god they could control. They made a calf that depended on them for protection and movement. The biblical description of that calf implies that it was a male.[4] Now I'm sure the writers of the Old Testament didn't know anything about American slang. But in their attempt to tell me how people once tried to make a god they could control, the writer said the people ended up with a lot of bull! A golden bull, but still a lot of bull! I seldom call my attempts to do the same thing today a lot of bull. I tend to call it maturity, or independence, or coming of age, or lots of other impressive things. But suppose it is still a lot of bull. The men who wrote the Bible mention the Second Commandment more than any other. Why?

They want to warn me of the danger of trying to "tame" or "domesticate" that ultimate authority we call God. Idolatry means attempting to use anything in the world—material, or intellectual, or spiritual—to control or manipulate God so I can get what I want.

These ancient people made a golden calf with their own hands. That sounds primitive. Then it dawns on me how easily I can look to the work of my hands for my salvation. When I do, I find religion turns into little more than a pep talk, to make me go out and work harder for good old materialism. As a result I worship my gold without even bothering to melt it down.

Nor do I make all the images I use to limit God's authority out of gold or silver or steel or wood. I have plenty of mental images to which I bow down. For instance, I have a mental image of custom and tradition. I have a strange way of confusing custom and tradition with God's moral authority.

4. Ruddlan Raber, *A Little God and a Lot of Bull* (Royal Oak, Mich.: Cathedral Press, 1972), p. 393.

What I call "Christian behavior" often means little more than customary behavior for white middle-class Americans. I have a strong tendency to confuse God's will with such customs. After all, tradition often represents the accumulated wisdom of people over a long period of time. I can't set it aside lightly. And suddenly I see why so many people resented Jesus so much. He went around saying many of their cherished customs and traditions simply did not please God at all. He went even further to say that they could not make an image of proper behavior and expect God to do what they wanted because they had behaved so nicely. They could not use their tradition and proper conduct to control God.

But even if I refuse to bow down to the image of materialism, or the image of tradition, I'm still not out of the woods. I also have a tendency to create "spiritual" or "religious" images. Ideas of God that cut him down to my size. For instance, I'd feel more comfortable with a God who for all his wisdom, now and then needs my advice.

So in hundreds of ways, I make images in an attempt to control God's authority. But suppose God remains forever different than any idea I have of him. Furthermore, suppose God's purposes run contrary to many of my strongest feelings and most cherished ideas. And suppose his authority does not depend on popular opinion. Suppose he does not have to work like a political candidate to create a favorable image in order to get elected and exercise some authority. Suppose God is God.

The New Testament keeps pointing to Jesus and saying, "Art, if you want to know how God exercises his authority, take a look at him." So I look and begin to see differences between how I think God should behave and how Jesus behaved. Jesus certainly had different ideas. He did the strangest things in the strangest ways. A man of his ability could have gone into the family business and made a killing. But he didn't.

He went out into the desert by himself. There on the threshold of mid-career, he wrestled with questions like, "Who am

I? What can I believe? What should I do with my life now?"
He came out of that experience with a strong sense of direction. The kind of direction that gave his life the ring of authority. Jesus began speaking with the authority of someone
in touch with truth who could put others in touch with truth.
People said no one ever talked with us like that before. Suddenly they heard the truth that unforgiving people can share
in God's forgiveness. Truth that says it's better to give than
to receive. Truth that says it's better to suffer wrong than
to go out and seek revenge.

Jesus traveled light. That never seemed to bother him or
to get him down. He did not have the best people for his
friends. Instead, people like Judas the thief, Simon the
revolutionary, John the bigot, Matthew the quisling, Mary
the prostitute became some of his closest associates. All of
them embarrassed his family. They thought Jesus had lost
touch with reality. They asked him to come home. And yet
those in poor health, and those out of work, and those who
had lost hope began to hear and see in Jesus a sane new
authority in a mad world. He told them that even at their
worst, when they admitted their need, they stood closer to
God than many of the proper types who made a big deal
out of social respectability and popular religion. And the
New Testament keeps saying, "God is like that."

Now that kind of talk didn't go down well back at the temple, or in the suburbs, or in the government offices. In those
seats of power, people soon saw in Jesus a direct challenge to
their authority. He challenged their authoritarian interpre-
tation of the law Moses laid down. To them it felt like Jesus
had turned all their values upside down.

Yet he never denied the validity of their law. He simply
said God and people come first. He healed on the Sabbath.
After all, how can a man say he loves God whom he cannot
see if he does not show compassion for a man he can see?
Jesus behaved as though laws are meant to serve people.
And people are meant to serve God and their fellows.

People in authority couldn't figure him out. But they saw
one thing clearly. If they could not control him, if he would

not back down, they had to get him out of the picture. Jesus simply refused to fit into their image of a proper authoritarian God. He couldn't even if it meant saving his life. So they framed him on charges of conspiracy and sedition, and murdered him. As though that would end it.

Yet Easter morning declares the irresistibility of the authority let loose among men in Jesus of Nazareth. Paul, writing out of his experience, said, "God was in Christ, reconciling the world to himself"—not in Buddha, not in Muhammad, but in Christ. Not in authoritarianism, religious or otherwise, but in Christ. And if that's true, then comparing religions may simply waste my time. One thing matters. God did something in Jesus. He openly declared his authority by reconciling black and white, rich and poor, ambitious and lazy, intelligent and stupid, hopeful and hopeless, sinner and saint, to himself. The authority of God came to life in a manger, hung on a cross, broke loose from death, and lives for all men. That marked the beginning of a new way of life in which I'm invited to share.

Yet I often sense myself hanging back. "Oh, Lord, this kind of talk threatens me terribly. Such a God could make unwanted changes in the way I see the world, the way I think about people and things. He may want to change my attitudes and my behavior. Honestly, I'd feel a lot more comfortable with a god who confirms what I already believe—a god I can use to protect what I've worked so hard for. I feel uncomfortable around a God who asks me to leave my treasures behind, and seek first his kingdom."

And then I hear the Lord saying, "Art, will you serve the God who made you, or will you serve the gods you make? It's a question of authority. And Art, your hopes for life lie in the answer you give."

When people come to join our church I ask them to answer in their own terms what having Christ as an authoritative point of reference means to them. One man wrote:

First, it signifies reconciliation and acceptance. Knowing that God has said "yes" to me is a continual source of joy and elation. Second, it means that my life has a new center, a new reference point, and an example worth following. . . . Third, it means that I must seek to become fully human in this world if I am going to continue experiencing the mystery of the living Christ. I must continually undergo redemptive dying, putting to death all within me which impedes human growth in order to experience resurrection of what I can truly be. Fourth, it means that *to love* . . . now has become my paramount value, my predominant purpose for living.

## QUESTIONS FOR REFLECTION AND DISCUSSION

1. Do you think God ever has the right to tell you what to do? Why? Why not?
2. How do you feel when God does not do what you think a good God should?
3. Are laws meant to serve people or are people meant to serve laws?
4. What kind of God would you feel most comfortable with?

# 3. CASUALLY YOURS

> You shall not take the name of the Lord your God in vain; for the Lord will not hold him guiltless who takes his name in vain.
>
> *Exodus 20:7*

Casually yours. That says it. Once flower power, assassinations, an army of young people in the streets laid siege to a culture. Some called the 1960s an adolescent decade for an adolescent culture.

Then suddenly, with the dawn of the 1970s, a sense of futility settled over it all. Many now standing on the threshold of their thirtieth birthdays have cut their hair and dress quite conventionally. Why not? What's worth protesting? Besides, if you dress and look like everybody else, you'll get into less trouble. Diogenes once pictured the "conversion" of a leading, protesting, long-haired Stoic. When the Stoic turned into a skeptic, he cut his hair and put on stylish clothes. He simply got fed up with fighting the crowd. After all, a man has to live, doesn't he?

Some years ago, Halford Luccock spotted an ad run by a large department store for a new fall coat. The caption under the ad read, "Casually yours." The ad went on to say, "This coat captures beautifully that fine air of informal unconcern. Casually yours." [1]

So much of life now seems to fit into that air of informal unconcern. Even in my search for deeper spiritual roots, God

---

1. Halford Luccock, *Unfinished Business* (New York: Harper & Bros., 1956), p. 139.

keeps getting shoved into that category—the category of spare time, something to think about after I've taken care of the important things, if I have time and energy left over. All those things Jesus said get put into the same bag with Sunday football or TV or sleeping in. "I'm casually yours, God."

A casual approach to God has all kinds of ramifications. For instance, I could start thinking of God as little more than another piece of Americana. Put in one bag the Declaration of Independence, the Bill of Rights, the hymn "America," repeated references to God in presidential inauguration speeches, and God begins to look like Uncle Sam. Add to this the inclusion of God in the pledge of allegiance to the flag, the ethos of good sportsmanship, belief in the soundness of our economic system, and you have what some people unthinkingly mean when they talk about our country being a Christian nation.

Suddenly I remember Moses and Pharaoh. Pharaoh, a massive historical figure. Talented. Powerful. With absolute civil authority. And wearing on his head a crown with the symbol of the sacred serpent. In Pharaoh the people of Egypt identified their god with their country. And Pharaoh accepted that. All at once I see why he so casually refused to acknowledge any order from Moses' God. "Who's god around here anyway?" Moses threw down his rod at Pharaoh's feet and it became a serpent. The symbol of Pharaoh's divine authority. Then Moses picked up the serpent and it became a rod again. But he picked it up by the tail. Most snake handlers pick up a snake right behind the head. Moses took this snake by the tail. As if to say, "Pharaoh, you want to know who's god around here? I'm going to take you by the tail and show you."

But how many today look to the Church as a place from which people go out into life to challenge and change the practices of government and redirect culture and reshape their civilization?

Yet as Senator Mark Hatfield said once to the president's prayer breakfast, "If we as leaders appeal to the gods of civil religion, our faith is in a small and excusive deity, a loyal spiritual advisor to power and prestige, a defender of only the American nation, the object of a national folk religion void of moral content. Lives lived under the Lordship of Jesus Christ at this point of our history may well put us at odds with the values of our society, abuses of political power, and cultural conformity of our church."

Suddenly, I hear, "Art, you shall not take the name of the Lord your God in vain. You shall not take his name in a casual, unthinking way."

When I hear the name *God* certain images begin to emerge on the screen of my imagination. Any person's name, like a little container in my mind, gets filled with all the memories and all the emotions I have in relation to that person. When I hear the name, that little container empties out and all those emotions and ideas and feelings flood across the screen of my conscious mind. An image emerges. I hear my wife's name and a whole flood of emotions gathered up over the years sweeps through me. Other names create completely different reactions.

So, the name *God* creates an image in my mind. That image may not be the right one. But for me, it contains the stories I've read and heard about a God who led some people out of slavery into a land of promise. He disrupted the whole fabric of society in the greatest nation in the world at the time to do it. Honest-to-God religion in persons and society proved more shocking and exciting than God denied.

These ex-slaves through prophets like Jonah discovered in God more than a national deity. He claims authority over all men. Their enemies were not his enemies. When the people became unfaithful to him, he remaind faithful to them. He would not accept religious performance as a substitute for personal and national justice. I am not simply my brother's brother I am my brother's keeper. He keeps asking questions like, "Art, where are you now? What are you doing here? And where is your brother?" So, when I hear the word *God* an image begins to emerge in my mind. It sensitizes my heart and spirit.

And for me, this God has a particularly human name.

Jesus. In Jesus, the image of God becomes concrete. Abstract ideas like beauty and goodness and truth suddenly have hands and feet and do things that have practical meaning for me. I see someone turning water into wine and saving the party. From then on, whenever he walked into a room, men cheered up. That's God to me.

God comes into my world unarmed, like a baby in the manger. Like Jesus on the Cross. And suddenly I see that force always indicates weakness and fear, never power. Slowly, I begin to understand that behind all the armies, and all the atomic stockpiles of all the world that we call power, stands fear and weakness. From any creative perspective, which is God's perspective, the use of force lacks the power to save us or keep us safe. Only absolute power held in control by absolute love can do that.

I see him on his knees with a towel wrapped around him and a basin of water in his hands. And I hear him saying, "Art, you know how powerful men in secular affairs like to lean on people and give orders and impress people with their importance. You're not to live like that."

The question isn't, "How much can you get out of life?" The question is, "What can you give? What can you contribute?"

Then I see him sitting in the guardhouse with a ring of thorns smashed down crossways on his head, his back red and raw, and the spit of the guard sliding down his face. No one seems to have remembered to write down what he said there. Maybe it all came out later in that agonizing cry from the Cross, "Father, forgive them, for they know not what they do." And again I sense that this God has no human enemies. However much he may hate evil, he refuses to hate the men who do it.

So in Jesus, I discover a God who takes people seriously. Not casually. Who gets involved in the events of our time. He simply refuses to remain a casual spectator, sitting somewhere beyond the blue, preoccupied with religious concerns and ceremonies.

Now if that's who God is, I have to ask myself what taking his name in vain means.

Of course I've had people tell me it means not to use God's name to swear or curse. And they have a point as far as it goes. When I use God's name I'm praying. When I use it to curse I'm praying God to damn something. Usually to damn some dumb thing like a hammer or a wrench. But sometimes a person. And that's bad. It asks God to go against his nature. God's not like that. He doesn't go around damning people. If Jesus is right, God loves people and came into the world to help them get themselves together. To put them in their right mind. To bring wholeness and health. If I ask God to damn people, I'm asking him to act in an ungodly way.

But that's the least of it. Picture this scene: Our ancient prehistoric ancestors have just begun to call each other by name. Suddenly they discover that if you call a man's name, he will stop and pay attention to you. Simply call his name and he will stop and turn around and maybe do what you ask. As though knowing a person's name gives you power over the person. That idea still lives. Many people still feel that if they use God's name, they have some kind of power over him to make him stop and do what they want him to do.

I've heard politicians casually using God's name to get a few votes. I've seen people worship God simply to meet other persons who can help them professionally or in business. In all kinds of ways, all kinds of people try to cash in on God's good name. And I catch myself trying to use God's name to get what I want done. No wonder Jesus said at the last day many will say to him, "Lord, Lord . . . and I will say to them, I never knew you. Depart from me!"

So today a lot of people simply refuse to use his name at all! A lot of them ache inside. Many want to get themselves together. They often feel like outsiders looking in on life. They wish they could believe in God, but frankly, the very word *God* shuts them down and turns them off. They can't bear the sound of it. They've heard so many argumentative, authoritarian, boring sermons that God's name sounds for-ever dull and revolting. Or they have an image of a timid reli-gious God loafing around the universe with the pathetic hope that we'll make use of him. As though I could casually switch

God on when I wanted him. And he'd stay out of my way until I called.

But who needs such a God? They couldn't care less.

Yet I keep hearing, "Art, you cannot treat God in a casual, offhand, unconcerned way." Suddenly I sense in God's name something like the sign that looms up on the back of a truck roaring down the freeway: "Danger—High Explosive." God's like that. God's not a toy. Something I can treat lightly. There's power there. And I always sense danger in relation to power.

King David once wanted to bring the ark of God into his capital city. The ark, that wooden box containing the stone tablets Moses brought down from Mount Sinai. It symbolized God's presence among his people. No one dared touch the box. Priests carried it on poles they slipped through rings at its sides.

But this time David had a new oxcart built and the priests sat the ark on it for the trip to the city. Somewhere along the way the cart swayed and it looked like the ark would fall off. A man named Uzzah rushed up and put out his hand to prop up the ark of God. He meant well. But he collapsed and died in the effort.

Uzzah felt God needed his support. As though God needed any prop to lean on. He underestimated God's power. And so do I. God can get along with us or without us. He is not God simply because people rally to his support. "If," said John Newton, "you think you see the ark of God tottering, you can be quite sure that it's due to a swimming in your own head."

Now this power of God broke loose in human history in Jesus. It began to change human nature and disrupt human society. It threatens some of my favorite ideas and pet prejudices. Yet I'm the kind of man who misuses God's name to get my way in family arguments.

Suddenly I hear the warning, "Art, watch out! You shall not take the name of the Lord your God in vain. There's power there. You can't keep going to hell without eventually getting there. Lies get exposed.

"Simply going to church may not make you a better person. It all depends. It depends on what you do and what you say because you're a Christian that you wouldn't do or wouldn't say if you weren't. Attend church? Read the Bible? Make a pledge? If that's all there is to it your religion can do you more harm than good.

"Remember how the prophet Amos said, 'Come to Bethel and sin against God. Go to Gilgal and sin still more.' Bethel? Gilgal? The most prominent places of worship of the day. It's as if the prophet said, 'Go to the First Presbyterian Church and sin against God. Go to the Baptist, the Catholic, the Bible or the drive-in church, and it's just as bad, if not worse.

"Religion by itself can salve your conscience and make you complacent in the face of monstrous falsehoods and long-standing injustices. But, Art, watch out. You can't treat God so casually. Men can promote and stage and popularize huge deceptions for a while. But in God's world 'truth crushed to earth will rise again.'

"Do you think you can get by simply preaching 'religious' sermons on Sunday morning and presiding over potluck dinners Sunday night? Don't you remember you live in a moral universe? You can't reduce God to a series of generalized, safe religious pronouncements. Nor can you shut God out of the political affairs of your world if you wanted to. He's not indifferent to the ethical crises—the failure of spirit of your time. And you need to say so and act as if you believed it."

So the warning against taking the name of God casually implies the corollary that I take it seriously.

And taking God seriously means that if I have some of the material resources of God in my hand and I use the means of competition to build up a profitable business or profession, I cannot use such resources to put my competitor on relief! If I do eventually I will come up against God himself. To take God seriously means that I cannot stamp, "In God We Trust" on coins and then trust almost completely in our military establishment.

Now, when men begin to take God seriously his power gets loose to change society and personal lives. I remember when Eugene Carson Blake, then Stated Clerk of the General

Assembly of the United Presbyterian Church, got his picture in the papers by refusing to obey segregation laws at a children's playground. A young church dropout in the San Joaquin Valley saw that picture. He began attending the Presbyterian church in his city. He told me later that he started taking God seriously because he saw a church willing to put its body where its mouth had always been. Taking God that seriously made a convert to Christ out of him.

When people dare to take God seriously and stand with him where the truth is, they do not always win, but sometimes they do win impressively against overwhelming odds.

And as I begin to take God seriously, I discover he's concerned not simply for changing personal life and the form of my state or economy. His concerns run far deeper. They have to do with the very framework of civilization.

At that point, I start trying to think of someone who lives in the same world I do. Someone who sees the facts but does not get depressed by them. He simply goes on being himself. He sees things in the long perspective of history. He makes critical judgments without becoming cynical or sour. Things change around him. Often for the worse. But he remains consistently human. I look for someone who has overcome the world. His success has not changed my world. But thinking of him changes me!

Jesus did the same thing for Peter and John and the others around him. They went through all the troubles and uncertainties everybody else of their generation did. Maybe they felt disappointed about that. Maybe they hoped Jesus would excuse them from it. But he didn't. He gave them no guarantee against disappointment, unfair treatment, or death. But he did give them himself. A Friend so given to his Father that he could stand up to anything and everything.

And the longer they lived with him the more they found themselves able to do the same thing. And I think I hear this same Jesus saying to me something like this:

"Art if you take God seriously you will not escape the troubles of living in a society that suffers from the mistakes of overambitious people, the violence of discontented people, the impatience of the young, and the failure of the old to understand.

"You may feel tempted to withdraw and make a safe little world of your own. I felt that temptation, but I didn't drop out. I couldn't. Nor can you.

"You may feel the struggle isn't worth the effort. My family told me to quit and come home.

"You may want to force people to go the way you think they ought to go. I felt that, but I didn't.

"You may get to the point where nothing makes sense and think that its a tale told by an idiot. So did I, but it isn't.

"So when you feel down in a trough look for someone who's riding the crest of the wave that threatens to bury you. Look for me—involved, but not overwhelmed, incarnate in flesh and blood, but not imprisoned by it. You'll find me if you really look for me. Maybe in a cab driver who gives you back some of the money because you gave him too much!

"And when you see me look through me to the Father, the brightness of whose being no dark cloud can hide. And that will cheer you up! Not with the cheerfulness of the bland or the blind. But with the joy of one who can stand at the center of a storm because he does not stand alone. The One who stands with him can take whatever comes because once he took it and did not fall."

## QUESTIONS FOR REFLECTION AND DISCUSSION

1. Do you think it's OK to use God's name as a swear word? Why? Why not?
2. What image does the name "God" create in your mind?
3. How do you feel about the statement, "A man has to live, doesn't he?"
4. Do you think it's ever right to try to use God to get what you want?
5. What does taking God seriously mean to you?

# 4. HAPPY DAY

Remember the sabbath day, to keep it holy. Six days you shall labor, and do all your work; but the seventh day is a sabbath to the Lord your God; in it you shall not do any work, you, or your son, or your daughter, your manservant, or your maidservant, or your cattle, or the sojourner who is within your gates; for in six days the Lord made heaven and earth, the sea, and all that is in them, and rested the seventh day, therefore the Lord blessed the sabbath day and hallowed it.

*Exodus 20:8–11*

As I left the house in the morning, my young son said, "Have a happy day, Dad." But living isn't easy. Life offers great possibilities, but so much can and does go wrong.

Some mornings, just getting out of bed takes real effort. A man sits on the edge of his bed staring at the floor. Each week ought to have at least one happy day. But he can't see anything ahead that makes the week look halfway interesting. He goes off to work wondering if it's worth the trouble. Worse yet, he has few pleasures that he gets much fun out of any more. And when he says, "I'm unhappy," he means, "I'm unhappy living the way I'm living." It takes more than the "happy hour" to get the grimness out of life. Oh, for a few really bright, happy days.

Moses thought he heard God saying the same thing. "You have six days to labor and do all your work. But the seventh day is a sabbath of the Lord your God."

That means I need time out. Time out to take eternity in. Time when I stop doing what I usually do. I need regular "time outs." Without them happiness and joy drain out of me.

Yet time gets away from me. Worse yet I often feel like I don't spend the hours of my life, others spend them for me. Time! I want it most but use it worst. I can't store it up. Nor can I substitute anything else for it.

Suddenly I sense that time belongs to God. It's just that I have a way of grabbing it out of his hands so I can keep it all to myself. Somehow that upsets everything. I seem to always have either too much or too little time. How can I redeem my time?

Here's a young mother. She has about everything she once thought would make her happy. Why does she feel so unhappy? She likes her home. She likes her husband. He seems to like her. They have money to pay the bills and enough left over to do the things they like to do. She watches her children developing into bright, healthy human beings. But children's clothes keep getting dirty. Even when they get into high school, they still make messes in the kitchen and living room and bedroom and bathroom. They fight and argue with each other. They annoy adults. When they do things young people ought to do, she can hardly stand it. She's not old. But she feels tired. Unsettled. Unhappy. She longs for a little space that will let some light in. A bright, happy day. Surely one such day a week isn't asking too much.

Then the other day I listened to a man in his sixties. Life had gone along relatively smoothly for a number of years. He had enough interests to keep him busy. But one day he went out and climbed a tree in the backyard to saw off a limb. Halfway up, he suddenly noticed the loss of physical agility and strength that he once had. Later that night, he got to thinking how four years ago he refinanced his house and borrowed on his insurance to invest in mutual funds. Today, he reads the pages of the stock market with a sinking feeling. He watches so much that he worked so hard for going down the drain. I heard sadness in his voice, a longing for happier days.

Most of us have responsibilities. We have problems to solve, promises to keep, children to support, debts to pay, a continually rising cost of living to meet. Few of us see much release from that for as long as we live.

Oh, I've heard that some people say they get great satisfaction out of their jobs. But I have friends who freely admit that they'd quit their jobs in a minute if they didn't need the money to pay the bills. So time drags by. Work bores us to death and leisure wears us out.

Events have a way of shaking the happiness right out of us. Subtly—sometimes quickly—life closes in. Sometimes people kid themselves into thinking that they'd feel happier if they could get married, or unmarried, or live in a bigger house, or in another neighborhood, or get the promotion, or get back suntanned from Hawaii. We long for some glimmer of light telling us that we're not permanently locked into our predicament.

A man and a woman fall in love. They begin sharing their lives together. And then suddenly the music dies. The world stops singing. Yesterday he held her hand and thought he held the whole world round. Somehow it ended before it began. They watched that dream go down behind the setting sun. A person can succeed at many things and still feel trapped and desperate, half dead, unable to move.

And now what? James and Jongeward in their helpful book *Born to Win* point out that many people feeling that kind of pain begin to live in the past. They shift the responsibility for their pain to others. They begin to say:

> If only I had married someone else . . .
> If only I had a different job . . .
> If only I had been handsome (beautiful) . . .
> If only my spouse had stopped drinking . . .
> If only I had been born rich . . .
> If only I had better parents . . .

Others, rather than looking back, try to look ahead. But they somehow postpone their lives by living in the future. They wait for some miracle, after which they'll live happily ever after. How wonderful life will be . . .

When school is over . . .
When Prince Charming or the ideal woman finally comes . . .
When the kids grow up . . .
When that new job opens . . .
When the boss dies . . .
When my ship comes in . . .

Others in contrast to those who look to the future for a miracle look to the future with constant dread. They continually worry about *what if:*

What if I lose my job . . .
What if I lose my mind . . .
What if something falls on me . . .
What if I break my leg . . .
What if they don't like me . . .
What if I make a mistake . . .

Such feelings immobilize people. They become repeaters of their own mistakes and often the repeaters of the mistakes of their family and culture. As James and Jongeward suggest: "Like the frog prince in the fairy tale, he is spellbound and lives life being something he isn't meant to be." [1]

Apparently our American way of life cannot guarantee happiness. Our constitution talks about "life, liberty and the pursuit of happiness." It tries to safeguard the pursuit of happiness. It does not guarantee happiness itself. Chasing happiness around is fun for a while, but the fun of it wears thin.

And how many of us who say we believe in God actually think he can give us much practical help in catching up with the happiness that eludes us?

Yet the first book of the Bible tells me, "Sarah said, 'God has given me good reason to laugh, and everyone who hears will laugh with me: God has made laughter for me!' "

I have several good friends who can make me laugh. Strange how I never thought of including God among them.

1. Muriel James and Dorothy Jongeward, *Born to Win* (Reading, Mass.: Addison Wesley, 1971), pp. 4–6.

It almost sounds sacrilegious. Yet suppose laughter begins with God? '

Why should I think God busies himself only with life's problems and tragedies and never with its funny side? Jesus began his Sermon on the Mount with a list of nine ways to be happy. That remained a central characteristic of so much that he said and did. He did not come to make people grim, but to release them and make them enormously happy. Nothing ever destroyed his good humor. Not even death. No one knows how Jesus did it, but Easter morning he sent some dispirited broken men out of an upper room stammering great good news.

How often I look at my problems and compute my chances of being happy without making God a very important part of that calculation. Suddenly I discover there is a world of difference psychologically between just plain god and the living God! When I lose sight of where that center is, I suddenly don't know where the boundaries are. At an ever-accelerating rate, I collect details, redouble my effort because I've lost my aim.

God wants people to live happy lives. That's the heart of it.

Forgetting that central reality can bring me quickly to grief. The American railroads started out in the transportation business. If they had stuck to that, they would today probably own the airlines. Unfortunately for them, they forgot that central reality. Instead of concentrating on transportation, they went instead into the train-building business. They fancied up the cars and put in extra plumbing. And today they face bankruptcy.

A few summers ago, near Santa Cruz, California, I noticed a large redwood tree fallen across a small canyon creek. A sudden windstorm and flood brought it down. Children used it for a natural bridge. I looked at the size of its trunk and wondered about its age. And I wondered why it happened to fall just now. Could anyone use it for lumber? Could they cut it up for firewood? Or would it just lie there to rot? I knew one thing for sure. Its life as a tree was over.

And then I looked at the huge trees standing all around. Some looked bigger and older than the fallen giant. Their roots still drank life from the soil. They could stand and grow for years. I thought how civilizations and cultures get caught in sudden storms. When the winds blow and the floods come, some get uprooted and blown over. It could happen to any culture. Cultures need to be rooted deeply in the soil of lasting spiritual value.

When Moses went up on Mount Sinai, I sense a man searching for guidelines for use in building a community of happy people. How could people sink their roots down deeply enough into spiritual reality to withstand the storms ahead?

When Moses came down from Mount Sinai, he brought with him one particular word that seemed to light up everything. A word he borrowed from the ancient Babylonian code. A bright, shining word: *Sabbath*. He used that word to introduce a radical new element into the life of his people.

"Remember the Sabbath Day . . ." As it stands in Exodus, this word says nothing at all about worshiping on the Sabbath. It says simply and directly, man should have at least one day in seven free from drudgery. He should insist on it. And what does that mean?

No one in all the world had come up with an idea quite like it before.

When Moses spoke these words everybody in the world, except a few privileged rich, worked from sunup until sundown seven days a week, week in week out. Men died in their late twenties or early thirties. Suddenly Moses heard a liberating word that broke the deadly cycle. Time off! Time to celebrate. Time for music, dancing, great food, parties. A day for joy and life. A little space to catch again the happy mood of paradise lost, the continuing joyous spiritual reality of the Garden of Eden. Time to enjoy ourselves, and enjoy our God, and enjoy each other, and enjoy the world we live in. Moses believed no society could long endure without this kind of spiritual foundation. People need time to get in touch with the joy of their spiritual origins.

Why do people crowd football stadiums and beaches and mountain resorts and golf courses on the weekend? Maybe in fumbling attempts to recapture somehow the happiness latter-day reformers drained out of the Sabbath.

The impulse to take the joy out of life comes straight from the devil. C. S. Lewis once commented that the devil never invented a single pleasure. Any "pleasure" in sin comes from a perversion of a deeper God-given joy. God gave me eating and drinking for my happiness. But gluttony and drunkenness will bring me misery and pain.

Now of course faith in God means more than fun and games. And yet the word *Sabbath* reminds me of the deep spiritual reality of God's joy and humor into which I need to penetrate more deeply.

Jesus enjoyed life. So much so that some called him a wine-bibber and glutton. He seemed to enjoy people. He also saw the dark side, but whenever he walked into a room, people cheered up. The socially prominent people of his day, the kind we call "the beautiful people," eagerly invited him to their dinner parties. They knew the party couldn't fail if Jesus came. He forever upset sober rabbis by sometimes carrying on like a groomsman at a wedding reception. And suddenly I sense that's how God intended people to live. That's his purpose for us.

I need time to remind me of the sheer joy of a paradise lost. Paradise, or the Garden of Eden, symbolizes a life in tune with God, full of happiness and joy and wonder. That's how Jesus lived. The mere sight of him unclenched the fist of Zaccheus from around his gold and made him a happy, generous person.

Sabbath reminds me I'm made for something bigger than working myself to death, or worrying myself to death, or running myself to death for fear I might miss something.

I can't identify the Sabbath with our Sunday. Sabbath started out as a day of rest and restoration. Sunday started as a day to celebrate the Lord's Resurrection. Then for hundreds of years Christians out of necessity used Sunday as a day of rest as well as worship. And the Sabbath and Sunday do have a relationship. But they aren't the same. With our five-day week most of us can observe both Sabbath and Sunday. Both days in their own way ought to help me get my spirits back.

Sunday worship should help me do that. Unfortunately not necessarily the worship I'm used to. G. A. Studdert-Kennedy once wrote a poem beginning,

> Our Padre were a solemn bloke
> We called 'im Dismal Jim . . .

Worship can become such a grim affair. I put on uncomfortable clothes and get myself into a decently uncomfortable state of mind in order to sit in decently uncomfortable pews.

Caricature? Perhaps. But then caricature simply exaggerates something real. And for a lot of us worship *is* uncomfortable and unhappy.

Yet I find little if any of this mood in the Bible. The ancient Jews had remarkably different worship services from any other religion in the world at the time. Their services included dancing, drama, great shouts of joy and singing.

The Jews kept saying, "Make a joyful noise to the Lord." Why not? If God means to set me free from my sins and fears so I can laugh again, who am I to drain the happiness out of worship by always singing sober hymns and listening to dull sermons? Why should we follow the same dull routine till it bores us out of our minds and drives our children straight out of the door? The impulse to put worship into a straight jacket and take the happiness out of it comes straight from the devil.

Of course worship will have incisive sobering moments. But Jesus seemed to seize worship as a golden opportunity to keep his soul alive. It gave him a chance to examine his life and times in the light of his God so full of joy and justice.

Now that kind of experience has a way of changing life's questions. It can release me from the devastating futility and boredom of unlimited self-expression. Six days a week I tend to worry about how much I can get out of life. I need at least one day, a little space to begin wondering about what I'm living for. That's a different question. I need time to ask, "Have I gotten off center?" "If so, where?"

Six days a week I tend to look around for something interesting and exciting to do. I need at least one other day to wonder where other people hurt and how I might help them.

Worship can help me see my life and my society as God sees it.

Suddenly I see God in the thick of the political and social turmoil of my time. And all at once I sense our founding fathers may have seen the same thing. Getting involved with God where the action is was the happiness they talked of pursuing. Not simply the private happiness of home and backyard, but the public happiness of involvement in the whole body politic.

At worship I discover social structures that favor the rich and powerful displease God. At worship I discover that policies, however disguised, which tend to slow down or reverse racial equality, grieve God. In the light of that, I find myself wondering why the richest 10 percent of Americans make more than the poorest 50 percent. Worship helps keep alive within me the glad purposes of God for the fulfillment of all people's lives. Jesus seemed to sense he needed that kind of worship to keep his soul alive.

I suppose most people have some kind of interest in God. Most people have some kind of interest in food. But the similarity ends there. If I miss a meal, I get hungry. But if I miss a worship service, I do not necessarily feel a stronger urge for God. Miss a meal and I want more food. Miss worship and I do not want God more, I want him less. Faith in the importance of God dies not by conviction but by disuse.

Jesus felt he needed worship as much as he needed fresh air, food, and water. So do I. I need worship on Sunday. I also need some relaxation, some fresh air, a little exercise, a lot of fun. And I find I cannot treat worship more casually than I treat any of the others.

I've begun to find happiness is not haphazard. It doesn't drop out of the sky by accident. People who think that happi-

ness falls down accidentally like rain forget that even rain
does not fall accidentally. It falls as a result of certain realities.

Happiness comes as a result of wholeness. Or *holiness*. That
word sounds terribly religious. But it means health. And that
helps me strip away sophisticated calculations about how
much religion I really need. Wholeness means betting my life
on the love of God. A lot of my friends say, "Art, you don't
have to go to church to do that. You can worship God anywhere."

Of course. A man can worship God anywhere. Someone
has suggested that it's possible to worship God when you're
trying to get off the deep rough beside the fifteenth green.
Maybe that's possible. I know I can't pull it off. I know that a
man watching a football game on Sunday may be just as self-
centered as a man taking communion. It's just that the man
watching the game on TV might pay no attention to his con-
dition and do nothing about it.

So when people tell me they have a strictly private relationship with God, I wonder where they got that idea? Certainly not from the Old or New Testament. Jesus never estab-
lished isolated Christians. He got twelve men together. He
did it on purpose. He knew these men would discover the
joy of the Lord together, not in isolation. He saw a community of faith as a requirement of human wholeness and happiness. I need the Church.

Leslie Newbigin in his book *The Household of God* compares the beginning of the Church with striking oil. When a
prospector goes out and stikes oil, it sometimes comes up a
gusher. The gusher often catches fire and burns for days. But
later on, there's no place for that kind of display. The oil gets
pumped through pipes and refineries and settles down to a
steady supply of power.

Now the Church began something like that on the day of
Pentecost. The earth shook, men saw fire. The great good
news got preached in a way that men of every language
could understand. The incident made a terrific impression on
the city. And when Peter finished trying to explain what had

happened, he asked people to do a very ordinary thing. He asked them to join the Church. And they did. Three thousand of them.

Peter realized that the powerful, joyous expression of God's presence could dissipate into nothing unless people found a way to channel that power productively. So he encouraged three thousand of them to join with him in that process. Christianity began, not as a disembodied kind of spiritual movement. It began as a mighty happy life in a visible institution. The first Christians saw no option to that. To say I believe in Jesus and not in the Church is like saying I believe in music and not in orchestras, or that I believe in worker's rights, but not in unions, or that I believe in education but not in schools.

This old institution for all its defects helps me remember whose I am. Its worship does not always reflect the quality of joy and happiness I believe that God has let loose in the world. But often it does point to a more basic joy than simply "living the good life." I could get bored with that.

## QUESTIONS FOR REFLECTION AND DISCUSSION

1. Do you think going to church on Sunday is important? Why? Why not?
2. What do you have too little time for?
3. How would you define happiness?
4. Do you think your personal happiness and God have anything to do with each other? Why? Why not?
5. What connection if any do worship and happiness have in your experience?

# 5. GETTING THE PERSPECTIVE

> Honor your father and your mother, that your days may be
> long in the land which the Lord your God gives you.
>
> *Exodus 20:12*

"The family is the worst thing one can imagine until one tries
to imagine something better," says Lawrence Fuchs, chairman of the American Studies at Brandeis University.[1] From
his perspective, young people have experimented enough
by now to realize it. Communes, with exceptions like the
Israeli *kibbutzim*, which maintain monogamous marriages
and provide time for parents to be with children, have failed,
says Fuchs.

As a result of such failures, more and more people turn to
where it all started, the family.

Still I see families racked by anxiety, frozen by lack of
communication, disrupted by dishonesty, teetering on the
brink of disaster. People in these homes get lost in neurotic
individualism, selfish hobbies, subtle aggressions, and money
meanness. They long for a new perspective.

Somewhere along the line someone sold them a contradictory and fraudulent set of values. As Harvey Cox says, "They
have been whipped into zealous profit-making and accumula-
tion (thus rending man from woman and parent from child)
and taught, at the same time, that the family should be a

1. Joanne Norris, "Families Back in Style," *Long Beach Independent-
Press Telegram*, 25 October 1972, p. A-23.

sunny island of warmth and bliss in a cold sea of cruelty and competition." [2]

And now the women's liberation movement complicates the picture. Some women feel like failures if they stay at home and rear children. Yet the same movement urges fathers to assume more responsibility in child care. That perspective helps.

Yet in some homes, children have parents running scared. In other homes, children live at the mercy of their parents. What kind of perspective will help young and old live together as maturing persons?

A lot of us fit into both the child and parent category. We have children living at home and we have living parents. To just such people, Moses said, "Honor your father and your mother."

To whom did Moses first address those words? To children? I doubt it. Most of the people standing at the foot of Mount Sinai that day were in the prime of life. People in their middle years who always carry the heaviest responsibilities. Not children, but fathers and mothers, aunts and uncles, and grandparents. Moses has a word primarily for adults.

What did he mean when he said to grown people, "Honor your father and mother"? I've seen adults seize this commandment and use it like a club to beat their children over the head with.

At a breath of criticism or independence on the part of a child they appeal to the Fifth Commandment. They demand constant gratitude for having done no more than their biological and legal duty. They feel they could monopolize the lives of grown children "in return for all I went through in bringing you up."

But Moses, when he said "honor" used a word that meant basically "to take seriously." It's as though he said, "Look at the people you live with. Take them seriously. That's critical. That will help you get the kind of perspective you need to live together."

2. Harvey Cox, "An American Family," *Christianity and Crisis,* 30 April 1973, p. 80.

Now that understanding of the word "honor" opens up whole new vistas for me. Suddenly I see that when my teen-aged sons look at me critically, they have begun to take me seriously. And they have begun to take themselves seriously.

But then comes the hard part. The part when I usually get defensive. I often get uptight when my children reject my views. How can they possibly take me seriously and not see things as I see them and think as I think? Should I let my boy waste his money? Or do I have a responsibility to see that he spends it in ways I think reasonable?

One incisive event recorded in the New Testament helps me get a sense of perspective on all this. Something happened between Jesus and his parents when Jesus entered his teens. And I always like to check his experience out against my own.

Every year Jesus had gone with his mother and father and aunts and uncles and cousins up to Jerusalem to celebrate the Passover. He camped with them outside the city in tents and went into town for the celebration. This year as usual, when the celebration ended, Mary and Joseph took down the tent, packed everything up, and with all the others headed back to Nazareth. No doubt they assumed Jesus had joined his cousins somewhere else in the caravan for the trip back.

However, at the end of the day when they stopped to camp for the night, no Jesus—no Jesus anywhere! He had simply run off without permission. And I know how uptight that makes a parent feel.

In the morning, Mary and Joseph headed back to Jerusalem. For three days, they walked all over that city looking for their irresponsible boy. Anything could have happened to him. Anger and fear tied their stomachs up in knots.

Finally they found him in the temple. There he sat, asking the professors questions they had trouble answering, and giving answers they could not question. I can see Mary breaking right into the circle and hear the edge in her voice when she said, "Son, why did you do this to us?"

The young boy looked up and said, "Mother, Dad, didn't

you know I have to be in my Father's house and about my Father's business?"

What had happened?

Apparently, that particular year, young Jesus sensed he had to begin developing an identity of his own. So for three days, he took charge of his own life. He got his own food. He looked for a place to sleep. And he went to the wisest men he could find and questioned them about life and its meaning.

It took nerve for a young boy to do that. Jesus knew what his mother and father expected of him. But suddenly he also knew he would have to begin making a break with his parents in order to test his own ideas, his own values, and enter into his own life.

That whole process creates tension. It created tension in the home of Jesus. It creates tension in my home. Tension over such things as, "When will you be home tonight?" Young people and parents at such times need the kind of perspective that allows them all enough room to establish themselves as developing persons.

Now this story of Jesus ends with the phrase, "He went down with them and came to Nazareth and was obedient to them." Does that mean he simply went home and began to take their orders again? I doubt it. It does mean Jesus recognized he had to resolve the tension between his need for his parents and his independence of them.

Out of that grew his understanding of how a man can be totally himself and yet completely responsive to his Father in heaven.

That kind of discovery on the part of young people requires something of parents. If a child cannot believe in people whom he can see, how will he ever believe in God whom he cannot see? So Jesus went down to Nazareth and took his parents seriously enough to listen to them, and evaluate the guidance they gave him.

For parents, that raises a whole lot of issues. For instance, I know people who find teen-agers physically and emotionally

in their way. Because they have budding teen-agers still living at home, they can't do everything they want to do. A
surprising number of adults simply do not like teen-agers. Oh,
they may worry about them or laugh at them, but they find it
hard to like them. Almost anyone can love a baby. But let
that baby grow on into adolescence and strange things happen to the feeling of adults.

What kind of an adult can a young person take seriously?
In trying to get a perspective on this, I hear a lot of talk
about authority and permissiveness or strictness. Should a
parent be strict or permissive? Obviously, both! But far
more basic than either strictness or permissiveness is a perspective that promotes the development of people. A perspective that goes beyond using orders or gimmicks to maneu-
ver teen-agers into doing what manipulative parents want
them to do.

Sometimes a conscientious parent wants his children to
have exactly what he enjoyed as a young person. Like the
man who had a few too many drinks. He woke up in the middle of the night with his mouth on fire. So he called his wife,
"Honey, get me some ice water." He drank it and said,
"Honey, this is so good, go wake up the kids and give them
some of it." So as Ruskin once said, "A lot of young people say,
'You are like all my other friends. You want to do me good
in your way, not mine.'"

My children need to develop a strong inner structure in
their own lives. To do that, I feel they need the security of a
home where they can try out new ideas for size, without fear
of embarrassment or humiliation. They also need to know
how I feel about essential matters. And they need to see my
convictions spelled out in my behavior.

I become unbelievable and lack authority to the degree
that I confuse essential matters with nonessentials. I may have
strong opinions about the length of my son's hair. It could
become a major issue around the house assuming the propor-
tions of an essential moral issue. But then suppose my son
thinks getting an education in order to earn as much money
as he can is more important than Jesus Christ. I could just

sit back and let that go by as a nonessential matter. The issue isn't strictness or permissiveness. I can cop out on my kids either way.

Jesus had a kind of mature authority about him that people found hard to describe. But they felt it. And they saw it. And it set them free. My children need to see something like that in me.

Jesus sat down with people and spoke quietly about things he knew from his experience. He never offered them a secondhand faith or warmed-over ideas.

He knew that murder grows out of inward hate. Hatred pulls the trigger. He said so. He knew the act of adultery grows out of an internal dislocation and the treatment is at the point of that inner dislocation. And he said so. He knew that public worship can become simply a show. What really mattered happened behind the closed doors of a man's inner life. And he said so.

He knew that so many of the things I love—my car, my boat—will never love me, even if I sell my soul to possess them. He knew my interest in money and my interest in God will sooner or later conflict. One or the other will get the upper hand. He knew I don't have to worry about the future, but until I can trust my Father, I'll never feel secure. Jesus knew his Father. He knew he could trust him, even though he did not always understand him fully.

The authority of Christ's life does not come from a club or a threat. He did try to clarify essential issues. He pointed out the difference between a man who built his house on a rock and another man who built his house on sand. But he never held a club over a man's head, threatening him to behave a particular way.

Nor did he appeal to tradition for his authority. Of course, he understood his tradition. It contributed to making him the person he was. But he went beyond it and often contrary to it.

Nor did he speak as a trained expert. He did not have a theological degree. Yes, he turned to the Scriptures often. But he never said, "This is true because the Bible says it."

What kind of authority did he have? The kind that has the

courage to stand up and say: "Out of my experience of God, this is the way things really look. Come and see for yourself."

He didn't argue. He spoke with the authority of a man with firsthand experience. He had a depth and wisdom that came to him from a firsthand experience with his Father.

Now that kind of authority still sets people free. It makes a tremendous impression. I get tired of the authority of the past. All my life I've had teachers who went by the book. If you asked them a question, they had to look it up and see what Leviticus or Buddha or Mao said. I get tired of that kind of authority. No wonder a college student at the end of a lecture on philosophy asked the professor, "Yes, professor, but what do you believe?"

I get tired of the authority of the club and the threat. I even get that in some churches. Rigid churches that tell me, "This is the law of God; if you don't obey it as we tell you, you're out, and when you're out, you're lost." Thousands have dropped out of church, tired of that kind of authoritarianism.

Different from all this, Jesus made just one claim. He simply claimed what he said was true. And he said it in the quiet kind of way of a man who knows. I hear him saying to me, "Art, you may not agree with me. You may see things quite differently. But out of my experience of God, this is the way things are."

And then he holds out to me standards far higher than anything I have dreamed of. He tells me I am expected to love not only my friends and neighbors, but my enemies! And there's something enormously appealing about the sheer audacity of a person who dares to say that.

As a parent, I need that perspective. If I claim authority and have a club in my hand to prove it, or if I appeal to the way they did things when I was a boy, and if I make no great appeal to a higher idealism, what intelligent child would honor such authority?

I find I can't order my children around and expect them to appropriate the values of God. But neither can I expect them to pick up these values by osmosis. I have found no substitute for doing the hard work of working through my own faith and sharing that growing and developing experience with my children. I find Christ an essential matter of life. I do not see him as an elective course in the school of living. But how will my children ever take that seriously unless I'm willing to wrestle through with them what it means for me to believe in this Christ, and how that faith shapes my attitudes and my behavior?

They need to know how my faith in Christ affects the value I give to money. They need to know what I will do to get it. They need to know what purposes I will use it for and why.

I have found that before they will listen to me, I have to listen to them. So, over the years, I have asked them what they think about older people, what they think about sex, what they think about money, what they think about war, what they think about drugs, what they think about the Church, what they think about Jesus Christ.

I didn't always find it easy to listen to them without losing my cool. But as a result of that process, I now find they have begun to ask me, "Dad, what do you think about war; what do you think about the distribution of resources in this world; what do you think about marijuana; what do you think about Jesus Christ and the Church?" They may not accept what I say I know, but now they want to know it.

People respond to authority because they can't live without it. Sure, we all go through periods when we like to do our own thing, irrespective of anything else. But before too long, I learned I couldn't live in this crowded world without authority vested in someone.

And I discovered God is not the kind of person who goes around the world issuing orders and expecting rigid rules to make me good. Nor did he leave me to myself thinking I will shape up on my own. Rather, he put himself, body and soul, on the line at the crossroads of life in Jesus of Nazareth.

I don't think we need tougher rules. Apparently, neither did God. I think we do need people who will dare to gain a new perspective of themselves in the light of Christ. People who will dare to share with their children in God the beginning of wisdom and its end. Then we can begin to experience the joy of our salvation together.

## QUESTIONS FOR REFLECTION AND DISCUSSION

1. How do you remember your father and mother?
2. Do you see any connection between honoring parents and the authority of parents?
3. In what sense do you take children seriously?
4. Do you have trouble talking with children about your deepest feelings? Why? Why not?
5. Do you think family ties are getting stronger or weaker today? What is causing them to get stronger or weaker?

# 6. THESE KILLING TIMES

You shall not kill.
*Exodus 20:13*

The 1972 California ballot carried an initiative asking voters to authorize the legislature to reinstate capital punishment. Wednesday morning after the election, a woman told me, "Art, I stayed up past midnight trying to make sense out of that."

We've all heard the words, "Thou shalt not kill." Nothing wishy-washy about that. A simple, direct, straightforward statement. No beating around the bush, saying, "Perhaps it would be better if you didn't," No. "Thou shalt not kill." A child can understand it. That ought to clear things up for people caught in these killing times. But does it?

An old Quaker once took those words literally. He ordered his whole life as a strict pacifist. Then, late one night, he heard the floorboards creak downstairs. Someone had broken in. Quietly, he crept out of bed, grabbed his flashlight and hunting rifle, sneaked downstairs and came up behind the thief just as he made for the window. The old Quaker shouted, "Friend, I would not harm thee for the world, but thou art standing where I am about to shoot."

"Thou shalt not kill." Ever? Anything? For any reason? These words seem to burst at the seams with meaning for our killing times. They suggest a lot of unfinished business for human civilization.

Albert Schweitzer literally believed men should not kill people, or animals, or bugs, or insects. Vegetarian friends of mine ask, "Art, how can you say you believe in God and kill for food?" But I walk away wondering what a vegetarian thinks he is doing every time he slices a tomato for lunch. The question is, what kind of life and which life do you take? Some years ago, Dr. Elton Trueblood in *Foundations For Reconstruction* asked, "Will I kill the lice which carry the typhus germ, or will I let the typhus germs kill the people?" That presents me with the choice of which life I shall take. Suppose I can kill the lice and refuse to do so. By trying to avoid the issue, don't I really say, "I value lice more than people?" And yet the command says, "Thou shalt not kill." Period!

But killing seems so much a part of life. Birds eat insects. Cats kill mice. Jesus ate fish by the Sea of Galilee. In spite of this apparently clear command, I find myself faced not so much with choices between good and evil, as with choices between evils. Should I try to take all the fight out of my children? Did Jesus sin in driving the money-changers out of the temple? Why do Israelis fight Arabs? Why do men, whatever their religion, seem tempted to kill whenever several of them want the same thing? What about military killing? What about judicial killing?

Dr. William Ramsay says he likes to ask his philosophy students at King College this question. "Suppose I killed that beautiful coed in the second row. Have I sinned?" He reports that most classes lapse into silence for a moment, and then answer: "It all depends." Dr. Ramsay continues, "If I'm driving along in a fifty-seven-horsepowered Opel and I see her, and I deliberately run her down and kill her, I sin. If, on the other hand, she whips down the hill on her skateboard, shoots right out in front of me without warning at the intersection, and gets killed in spite of my frantic efforts to avoid hitting her, I've killed her just as dead. But in that case, I'm not likely to get accused of murder." [1]

That seems to suggest that in killing, the motive counts. But the coed remains just as dead. So others say, motives don't count at all, only actions and results.

1. William Ramsay, "Principle: What Makes an Act Right?" *The Presbyterian Outlook,* 18 September 1974, p. 13.

And then I remember that story of the Good Samaritan. The story of a man who got mugged and beaten within an inch of his life on his way from Jerusalem to Jericho. A priest came along, but didn't do anything. A Levite stopped to look, but not to help. Finally, a man of a different race and religious and political outlook took the time to patch the injured man up and get him to where he could get some help.

As I think about that, I begin to wonder what that "Good Samaritan" would have done if he had come down the road twenty-five minutes sooner than he did. Suppose he had caught the thugs in the act of beating the man up. Would he simply have passed by on the other side and not gotten involved? Wouldn't he then have become an accessory to the fact of this man's murder? Is there any difference in restraining someone bent on violence, and the dropping of tons of bombs that destroy thousands of people indiscriminately?

In the Garden of Gethsemane, Jesus seemed to wrestle with exactly that kind of issue. He sensed that somehow or other, he had at his disposal the kind of power he could use to blast his enemies out of existence—this Jesus who taught me to love my enemies. Today, the whole world remembers how he chose the Cross. Most of us will kill in order to save ourselves. And here's God's son dying in order to save our lives.

The word translated "kill" in the commandment "Thou shalt not kill" comes from a Hebrew root which means "to commit murder." And I understand murder to mean "the unjustified taking of human life, the unjustified liquidation of my enemy."

That ought to clear things up. But in the light of the Cross of Christ, how do I justify taking the life of my enemy? I somehow can't shake from my mind that general's comment after taking a village in South Vietnam, "We had to destroy it to save it." But what relevance did our best national intentions have to widows and orphans and the homeless in Vietnam? I begin to see how if amoral stupidity gave us Watergate, amoral brilliance gave us Vietnam. The common factor in both being the amoral lust for and use of power.

So in these killing times, I get to wondering about war in

general. Can I ever justify it? Not long ago, Blanche Wieson
Cook pointed out in the Los Angeles *Times* how President
Eisenhower thought war an outmoded strategy. He prayed
that World War II might be "the last civil war to tear civilization apart." Eisenhower feared militarism so much that in his
first term he reduced the size of our army and cut military
spending by over $10 million. Cook goes on to tell how in an
article for the *Saturday Evening Post* in 1963, Eisenhower
called for the reduction of U.S. troops in Europe to one division. Let any political leader suggest such a reduction today
and he almost sounds traitorous. Eisenhower believed that
armaments would lead "at worst, to atomic warfare; at best,
to robbing every people and nation of the fruits of their own
toil."

During a press conference at the time of the Berlin crisis in
1959, someone asked Ike, "Mr. President, are you prepared
to use nuclear war . . . to defend free Berlin?"

He answered, "Well, I don't know how you could free
anything with nuclear weapons." When Peter Lisagor of the
Chicago *Daily News* wondered if there was "an in-between
response," Eisenhower replied: "I think we might as well
understand this—might as well all of us understand this—de-
struction is not a good police force. You don't throw hand
grenades around streets to police the streets so that people
won't be molested by thugs."

Can the systematic killing of human beings solve conflicts
between nations? I can't imagine any follower of Jesus not
agreeing that war is tragic and ought not to happen. Of
course, Jesus nowhere suggests that evil must go unchecked.
On the basis of that, I suppose some Christians feel they can
justify particular wars. But in the light of the Cross of Jesus,
others feel they cannot fight in any war. And surely, no follower of Jesus can think with a very easy conscience of killing
a person made "in the image of God."

But the issue does not stop there for me. What about the
lady struggling over her ballot and her vote on capital punishment? Being the vengeful kind of sinner that I am, I have to
ask myself, "Art, how does the whole idea of capital punish-

ment stand up in the light of your understanding of the infinite value of all human life?" I know sincere Christian people have often pointed to the Old Testament for justification of the idea of capital punishment of a convicted murderer.

Then my mind goes back to the very first book in the Bible. The poetic imagery of the first few chapters suggests that up to a point no one had yet seen a man die. Then Cain swung his club. Abel, his brother, fell to the ground and Cain stormed off the field. Suddenly, he looked back over his shoulder. Abel hadn't moved. Cain wondered why he lay still so long. Why didn't he get up? Why did he look so pale? "Abel! Abel! You were full of life this morning. Oh, my God . . ." Little by little, it dawned on Cain that he now had no brother. The earth swam around him.

Suddenly, God appeared on the scene. Cain stood with blood on his hands. And God did a surprising thing. He put a mark on Cain. Why? Cain stood convicted of his crime. But God didn't execute him. Instead, he put a mark on Cain so that no one else would kill him! And all that happened long before the writing of the Book of Leviticus and latter-day Jewish laws.

So when people point to the Old Testament to support the idea of capital punishment, I find their arguments falling apart. I discover that once you follow the Old Testament law to the letter in killing of convicted murderers, the same Old Testament tells us to kill adulterers, and to kill all those who stray from orthodox Old Testament religion. The whole premise of capital punishment gets shaky at that point. Suddenly, I sense the significance of the New Testament statement that it is the letter of the law that kills and the spirit that makes alive.

I don't see how anyone can naïvely apply one part of Old Testament law to the twentieth century and forget the rest. And I have yet to find a proponent of capital punishment who would like also to demand capital punishment for adultery or for anyone who does not practice orthodox Old Testament religion.

But I've had other people say: "Art, we justify capital

punishment on the basis that it deters crimes of violence." So
I looked for evidence of that. But I found by looking at the
statistics provided by the FBI that you cannot tell by the
homicide rate in contiguous states which ones have capital
punishment, and which ones do not, if you don't know ahead
of time. I have also discovered that states and nations which
have abolished the death penalty report that abolition did
not result in an increase in the murder rate. Those states and
nations which restored the death penalty after a period of
abolition reported that restoration did not result in a decrease
in the murder rate.[2]

So, with all these things going through my mind and heart,
the very words *capital punishment* suddenly begin sounding
like a contradiction in terms. Punishment implies correction.
It assumes the correctability of a person or situation. And I
begin asking myself, "If you kill a man, don't you take away
any possibility of his correction or salvation? And didn't Jesus
come to seek and to save, to redeem, to reconcile, to make
new even the most hopeless of sinners?"

Nor does the whole killing issue stop with that. What about
abortion? I believe that through scientific birth control, God
offers women new freedom and new self-determination as
persons. A wife now has the right to release from worrying
about having unwanted children. In this sense, birth control
becomes, I believe, a part of the liberating good news of the
Gospel of Jesus Christ. But I also believe that freedom can
become license. So I have to ask myself, can I justify the killing of life that has hardly started?

Granted, in some instances, abortion may be therapeuti-
cally necessary. However, Barbara Ward comments:

Although abortions in the early stages of pregnancy—when the fetus
is still going through the amoeba and fish-like stages of pre-mam-
malian life—are physically nearer to the innumerable early mis-
carriages which occur in nature and do not involve killing an already

2. *Uniform Crime Reports,* Department of Justice.

clearly human infant, a human life has started to stir and the issue of the sacredness of life is involved.[3]

I'm not sure I can make a choice between legalized killing through abortion and leaving women wretched with no "out" except through criminally incompetent and medically disastrous illegal practitioners. As with war, I'm left with a choice between evils. To protest legalized abortion is one thing. The real test comes at the point at which I must decide whether I am willing to go to work to get rid of the conditions that encourage the necessity of such legislation.

So this word "Thou shalt not kill" reminds me of how easily I get maneuvered into a postion where killing seems like the least of two evils, the best way out of a hard moral dilemma. Right at that point, I believe God has warned me, "Art, be-careful. Life is sacred, and I have created all men in my image. Watch out! Thou shalt not kill.

"You shall not kill singly or in mass. You shall not kill your contemporaries by impending incineration or generations still unborn by polluting the atmosphere and the earth."

Jesus once said,

You have heard that it was said to the men of old, "'You shall not kill; and whoever kills shall be liable to judgment." But I say to you that every one who is angry with his brother shall be liable to judgment; whoever insults his brother shall be liable to the council, and whoever says "You fool!" shall be liable to the hell of fire. So if you are offering your gift at the altar, and there remember that your brother has something against you, leave your gift there before the altar and go; first be reconciled to your brother, and then come and offer your gift. (Matthew 5:21–24.)

I hear him saying to me, "Art, the old law and the old traditions say, 'Don't murder,' but let me explain something to you. Murder starts way back in your attitude. When you have contempt for a man, for his race; when you look at a man

3. Barbara Ward, "The Question of Abortion," *The Presbyterian Outlook,* 30 October 1972, p. 9.

as worthless because of his point of view, you have already begun to kill him in your heart."

And I think back again to that story of Cain. Remarkable that the first two times God appears on the scene in human history in the Bible, he does not appear in church or in a religious context. He found Cain out in the field where Cain worked. He came with a question. Not a religious question. God didn't ask, "Cain, do you have any faith?" He asked, "Cain, where is your brother?"

I sense him coming to me with the same question. Not so much asking whether or not I have killed my brother, but do I know where he is. Have I chosen to ignore or neglect him?

So in my day, I hear the Lord asking, "Where is your brother? Art, what do you know about the boys hanging around your church who got into trouble with the law?"

"Not much, Lord. Oh, a few months ago, I tried to get something going for them, but my calendar was so full."

"Well, come and tell me. Did you know anything about the Arab refugees and the children who died of starvation last year?"

"No, Lord, how could I know about that? I only know what I read in the newspapers. I did hear of someone taking an offering, but I passed it off as another cry for money. Anyway, my taxes are so high."

But the questions keep coming. God seems to ask them about the whole of life. I shift my feet and feel that in spite of all my denials, in spite of all my admissions, I am a member of the whole human race. And God keeps asking me, "Art, where were you that night when one of my children needed help? Where is Abel, your brother?"

"God, I don't know where he is. I'm not responsible for him. I don't have time for him. I have enough troubles of my own that I can't handle."

But even as I speak, I sense within me a growing realization that every man on the face of this earth belongs to God. Whether he gets machine-gunned in South Africa, jailed in Hungary, goes unemployed in Watts, unvisited next door, he belongs to God. And I cannot ignore or repress or lay violent hands on him without violating someone who belongs to God himself. Whoever touches the life of any man touches the Lord.

God comes to us like that. In the flesh. Most people didn't recognize God in the flesh of Jesus. The priests didn't see it. Herod missed the point. Most of the Roman soliders couldn't see it. But Peter did. John did. A few did.

The cry coming from the hungry, the repressed, the poor, comes from the heart of God himself.

He's alive. He moves in the currents and crosscurrents of my world, calling for me and inviting me to join him as an agent of reconciliation, bringing my brother into his presence, in order that together we might share the life God offers.

Suddenly I see how partisan Christ is. He takes sides. He's for life. He's for the enlargement of every man's life. "I am come that you might live life . . ."

I lived for years preoccupied with my own life, my own salvation. In reading the New Testament I sense Paul did the same thing. What could he do to get things right with himself and right with his God? What excuses could he give for what he'd done or failed to do? None. Yet he had been zealous for God to the point of "breathing threats and murder."

Suddenly on his way to Damascus that preoccupation got wiped away. In a few days his eyes opened to a whole new world. The same old world of course. But now he saw everything so differently. He said he had become a new man in Christ. What did he mean? How can anyone get inside another person? He meant that the center of gravity in his life had shifted from wanting to save himself to wanting to save other people.

Paul didn't become a completely different person. He lived in the same body. His friends still recognized him. He had the same aches and pains, the same personality. He still carried the physical and emotional scars of his early history. But he did have new life.

The same Paul began to live in a different way. He now felt free from that terrible load of guilt, free to move to do things he knew the Lord wanted him to do. And he began to see

through things he had not seen through before. He saw
through the barriers that separated people, broke relationships, and made men mad enough to kill each other in one
way or another. He now saw that there are no Jews or
Gentiles, Greeks or barbarians, slaves or freemen: only those
who are in Christ and those who are not.

He soon discovered that he had a new inner strength to
carry burdens he had never carried before. Not his burdens.
The burdens of other people. He could go through things and
do things he had never dreamed of doing. Later he wrote,
"When someone becomes a Christian he becomes a brand
new person inside. He is not the same anymore: a new life
has begun" (II Cor. 5:17).

If there are to be such new men in our day they will look
very much like you and me.


## QUESTIONS FOR REFLECTION AND DISCUSSION

1. In what sense are we responsible for each other's life?
2. Is killing ever right? Why? Why not?
3. Do you think "You shall not kill" applies to the judicial taking
   of human life?
4. Killing in self-defense, as in war, may seem logical. How would
   you relate this commandment to self-defense situations?
5. How would you relate this commandment to the much debated
   subject of abortion?

# 7. GOOD GRIEF

You shall not commit adultery.

*Exodus 20:14*

My generation did not invent sex, adultery, or pornography. When people tell me, "Art, it wasn't like this in the good old days," I have a feeling they have simply found out too late what life has always been like. As for pornography, to me sex has always seemed a participatory rather than a spectator sport. A good thing that could come to grief.

Gail Sheehy in her perceptive article "Catch-30" in *New York* magazine noted that before one can establish real intimacy with a mate, or any other person one has to develop a reasonable sense of identity. Yet marriage often short-circuits young people's personal growth. He and she simply slip into acting as they "should" as spouses and parents. So together they light the fuse of midlife marital explosions by failing to achieve "genuine intimacy." The kind of intimacy that balances the act of giving oneself to another while still maintaining oneself.

Then as persons nearing forty they run up against the hard fact that they have stopped growing up and have begun to grow old. A man told me of one sure sign of approaching middle age. His wife decided to give up sex for Lent. But he didn't find out about it until after Easter!

So how can I develop a capacity for intimacy and still remain true to myself? How can I get beyond what Sheehy calls open-contract experiments with whimpering endings that keep so many people in a state of mess?

C. S. Lewis in *Mere Christianity* commented, "We grow up surrounded by propaganda in favor of unchastity. There are people who want to keep our sex instinct inflamed in order to make money out of us. Because, of course, a man with an obsession is a man who has very little sales resistance."

Strange, how such a good thing can bring such grief. A man took my hand at the end of a church service. "Art, I'd like to talk with you for about five minutes." After greeting other people, I met him outside the church door. I remembered him well. A little over a year ago I had officiated at the funeral of his wife. This morning, he introduced me to an attractive woman friend. But he looked troubled. They both did. "Could we see you for a few minutes sometime this week?"

Tuesday morning at 11:30 they both showed up at my door. I invited them in and they sat down. He slouched in his chair and began by saying, "We have a question. We really don't expect you to answer it, but we would like your opinion. Betty and I met some time ago and I guess you could say, fell in love. In the past few months, we have committed acts of adultery. We both belong to churches and we felt wrong about it when we did it, but we did it. Our belief in God drove us to asking for his forgiveness. But we love each other, and now Betty wants to divorce her husband. This whole adultery thing bothers us a lot. Especially Betty. We read in the Bible where Jesus said: 'They were told, "A man who divorces his wife must give her a note of dismissal." But what I tell you is this. If a man divorces his wife for any cause other than unchastity he involves her in adultery; and anyone who marries a divorced woman commits adultery.'

"Art, Betty is afraid that if she divorces her husband and we get married, every time we have sex, she would be committing adultery. What do you think? We need help."

Tears spilled out of the woman's eyes. I saw two grieving people in front of me and thought how our strengths and our weaknesses get so confused. Samson once thought he could cope with anything. He could rout a battalion single-handed. But something happened between Samson and Delilah that brought them both to grief. That doesn't make Samson any

worse than anybody else. It simply makes him a lot like the
rest of us. And suppose God had intended something far
better and grander for both Samson and Delilah. And for all
of us.

In the beginning God created something good. Sex. But a
lot has happened since to debase sex. However, human
sexuality has contributed significantly to the finest art,
poetry, and literature we have. In a sense, sex provides a
physical foundation for the highest spiritual life in us. The
ancient prophets had good reason for comparing the union
between husband and wife with that mystical union between a human spirit and the Spirit of God.

This view of sexuality takes sex beyond simply genital behavior. Why do so many couples who come to grief in their
sex lives treat it as chiefly a mechanical problem? Why do
they troop off to sex clinics to learn how to get more mileage
out of each other as sex stimulators? Because, somehow, they
do not see that one makes love not simply with his genitals
but with his self. Sexual experience as a means of communication and commitment gets lost.

Sex can become just another appetite, with little more
significance than taking a drink of water. So Harold Berg suggests, "By an interesting meeting of extremes, the inhibited
Puritan and the uninhibited libertine arrive at exactly the
same conclusion, that sex and love are unrelated." [1]

Right at that point, I hear, "Art, you shall not commit
adultery." Behind that statement, I hear someone insisting
that sexual intimacy and love belong together.

The kind of love that allows and encourages him and her
to develop as persons. That's easier for him than for her. He
can achieve proficiency in his work out in the world away
from home. There he can prove himself. She stays home
struggling to meet the demands of small children. Then somewhere around thirty she struggles with feelings of inadequacy.
He has moved on in his personal development and she feels

---

1. Harold Berg, *The Ten Commandments and You* (Philadelphia:
Fortress Press, 1964), pp. 62–63.

left behind. And he thinks so too. So he tells her to go back to school and get a degree in something or other. Maybe then she'll feel fulfilled and he won't have to worry about her problems. Unfortunately his advice comes because he cares more about his convenience than he does about her development. And she feels it. Both can see a lack of intimacy between them.

The word *sex* has become as controversial as the word *peace*. It all depends on who uses it and what he wants to say. A group of Methodists not long ago tried to come up with a consensus statement on the meaning of sexuality. In the process, they turned down a suggestion that said sex is "good fun." Sex, some said, was "beautiful" and even "holy" but certainly not "good fun"! Yet sexuality includes not only the biological facts, but also my attitudes, feelings, values, and spiritual views. As such it becomes a means of expressing my love or lack of love.

My sexuality only develops in an atmosphere of trust. Thats why I take seriously the warning, "You shall not commit adultery." Adultery means anything that would shake the confidence and weaken the trust of one person in another. Love requires commitment. That hits me full force when I stand in the shadow of the Cross. God made a commitment. Without taking anybody's advice he decided to love me unconditionally. And suddenly I sensed why the words, "As long as we both shall live," appear in the services of Christian marriage. A man and woman decide to commit themselves to each other as completely as they can. Each person decides to commit as much of himself as he understands to as much of the other person as he knows. That creates a relationship of confidence and trust. Both can now grow together as stronger and better people than either of them might alone. But the relationship will last only *if* it furthers both his and her personal development. That *if* is one of the biggest *ifs* I know. How many men at twenty think twice about their girlfriends' or wives' need for development?

Some people feel couples should stay together only as

long as they remain good friends. But how can such an arrangement even foster real friendship? Friendship itself relies on trust. Adultery means anything that shakes human confidence and weakens human trust.

The fact that one marriage in three ends in divorce adds little to the development of persons. An attractive young blond woman went to see her attorney. "I want to know whether or not I have grounds for a divorce."

"Are you married?"

"Yes."

"You have grounds."

I have no doubt that God puts some marriages asunder. How many others simmer along in bitterness for years, only God knows. Whenever Jesus spoke of marriage, he also spoke of divorce. Reluctantly, and with a sense of grief, he recognized some situations became so bad that divorce might be the lesser of two evils. He quoted Moses as recognizing that divorce might be necessary in some situations. But Jesus always emphasized the intent of marriage as a permanent relationship.

So the question isn't "Under what conditions can I justifiably get a divorce?" Such a break always involves grief and stands as a ruined opportunity. I hear the Lord saying, "Art, marriage goes beyond a conditional arrangement you can dissolve if the experiment entered into tentatively doesn't work out. That's why people make promises to each other in front of a congregation. Anybody in love might try to justify premarital sex by saying, 'We're already married in the eyes of God.' But for centuries, Christians have required a public, permanent, witnessed, unequivocal commitment. A commitment made to God and each other. Art, that kind of commitment gives you space and freedom to work out your personal humanity."

That's a spiritual reality I need to sink my roots into. I do need freedom and space to work out my identity. In its June 16, 1973, edition, *Newsweek* magazine featured an article on "Games Singles Play." I read it and thought how much I did

not envy those people. I have a sexual commitment that frees
me from always having to compete in some kind of sexual
sweepstakes. *Newsweek*'s editor commented:

There are players who score and those who strike out, yet for
both, a sobering degree of loneliness and *tristesse* seems to be built
into the rules. It is no revelation that the physically unattractive
and socially maladroit find the singles game a never-ending round of
rejection. But what does surprise is the prevalence of unhappiness
among the very singles who appear ostensibly to be living the
Mary-Tyler-Moore life. Gail Slabod, a curvaceous, twenty-five-year-
old Manhattan stockbroker, confesses that no amount of dazzling
the boys on the Fire Island beach can fill a gnawing emptiness in
her existence. "Sex has gotten so cheap," she told *Newsweek's*
Phyllis Malamud with a sad smile, "the biggest void in my life is
children. I may have one, even though I don't get married."

The longer that many "swinging" singles play their roles, the
harder it seems to unlearn the script, to break off the quest for new
conquests and the conditioned adjustment to a paucity of communication and commitment. Some finally suffer from a kind of battle
fatigue, a hunkering down in psychic bunkers! "You finally close
off the world," reports one Manhattan woman reporter, "You say
to yourself: 'Why should I go to that party? Why should I make
the ski scene? It'll just be the same lines, the same plastic hustling.' "

Her complaint is echoed by a bright Chicago secretary who will
soon turn in her key at International Village after a two-year stay.
"The whole scene begins to seem so empty, so contrived," she
says, "it's simply not the kind of place to grow up in. I'm ready for
the real world."

Any marriage has a hundred griefs that might prove any
experimental sexual relationship a failure. But when two
people commit themselves to each other as completely as they
can, it brings a security that sets them free.

But, let's face it. Life can get dull. Married life in particular. Not that either person deliberately tried to sabotage the
relationship. Neither may get drunk or play around. People just sometimes get to a place where their marriage feels
like it has begun to wear out, get monotonous, go nowhere but
downhill. Now what?

Well a person could say, "I still believe in marriage, but not to this person. I'll get a divorce. I'll see if I can do better the second time around."

But commitment is active, not passive. It means saying, "This is my marriage. It hasn't turned out the way I hoped it would. A lot of my dreams lie broken at my feet. But I have this marriage. I'm going to live with it and for it and give as much of myself as I can to it."

A marriage relationship does not have to get dull and monotonous. After all, I'm not the same person I was five years ago or ten years ago. Neither is my wife. I was one kind of person as a young husband right out of college. I'm a different kind of person today, with two children in college. My moods reach different heights and depths from year to year. My ideas and attitudes change. Furthermore, I'm a different person on vacation than I am at work. So is my wife. Besides that, I suddenly find myself at an age where I realize I may not attain some of the grand dreams I had as a younger man. And my wife and children have grown and become different persons with new, challenging interests.

André Maurois once described the process in terms of a man stepping out into his garden to look at a prize rose. The rose had a particular beauty in the morning, but another in the evening. What compares to an opening bud, fresh with dew? And yet a full bloom, late in the afternoon, has a beauty all its own. Any gardener knows the joys of the constant changes. Seen in this light, the relationship between a man and a woman need not get lifeless and unfulfilling.

The quality of commitment counts. God warns me against anything that would adulterate that.

Some time ago, Dr. Bryant Kirkland commented on reading a news story of a young couple who decided to walk home from a party on a warm moonlit night. They took a shortcut across a railroad trestle. On the way across, the girl somehow caught her foot between the track and the ties. She couldn't get it out. They struggled together, but neither of them could get her foot out. They heard the train coming. People watching from a farmhouse not far away saw the young woman wildly trying to push her husband out of the way and save his life. But eyewitnesses reported that he hung onto her and worked to the end trying to free her. They died together as the engineer frantically applied the brakes, throwing the engine into reverse in a futile effort to stop in time.

A sophisticated couple out in the suburbs read the story the next morning in the newspaper. This couple, in their search for maturity and freedom and fulfillment, had mutually agreed to practice extramarital sex. They read the story together over morning coffee. Then, they put the paper down, and looked searchingly into each other's eyes. Finally, the wife stammered, "Our trouble is that I don't really know if you would do that for me, or if I'd do it for you."

Isn't that the issue? The quality of our commitment. To God and to each other. The kind of love I have begun to discover in Christ comes with no strings attached and serves as a prerequisite to the fulfilling of my personal identity. And the fulfilling of that has a lot to do with all of the human relationships in my society.

I have just recently begun to discover how my commitment to the fulfillment of sexuality of all men and women has far-reaching social implications. Every man and woman ought to have an opportunity to develop a quality sexual life. But how can anyone manage it, crowded as many are into inner-city housing developments or living in rural tarpaper shacks without water, without work, without privacy? Under such conditions, marriage takes heroic efforts. Why should any society demand so much of its weakest and poorest?

Church people can safely and easily attack pornography and sexual perversion. But it's not so easy or safe to attack terrible public violations of greed and power that destroy men and women and deprive whole communities of their basic right to fulfilling sexual relationships within the bonds of human commitment.

If I really take "You shall not commit adultery" seriously, I may have to help reshape some of the institutions that make for unfaithfulness. So much in my time works against faith. So much works against commitment. Faith people have in each other will not maintain itself. Commitment and trust require continual care and vigilance.

## QUESTIONS FOR REFLECTION AND DISCUSSION

1. Some persons argue that sex outside of marriage is OK today. Do you agree? Why? Why not?
2. In what sense do you think sex and love belong together?
3. Do you think Christian wedding vows have greater or less significance today?
4. What kind of relationship do you think gives a man and woman the most freedom to develop as persons?
5. What things would you say are most important in making a marriage work?

# 8. GIVE AND TAKE

> You shall not steal.
> *Exodus 20:15*

Give and take. I live between these two poles. I began as a child, reaching out and taking things. No one taught me to do that. I came into the world on the take. A good instinct. I need to take if I'm to live. Furthermore, I take things that do not belong to me, sunshine, air, ideas. I'd die if I didn't. I need to take air. I need to take in sunshine. I own none of these things. Yet my life depends on my continuing to take them.

So, like sex, taking is a good thing. What I do with it makes all the difference.

"You shall not steal." When does taking become stealing? Suddenly I'm right up against the whole idea of ownership. My understanding of the difference between taking and stealing depends partly on my understanding of ownership.

I have an unhappy habit of defining stealing to suit myself. I won't steal—much. Rob a bank? Never! Clip the company for a few bucks on the expense account? Why not? "They ought to pay me a better salary anyway."

Not long ago, a man smashed up his car. His insurance broker told him to pretend he ruined his back. The man protested. But his broker said, "Everybody does it." The company expects it. Insurance experts estimate 75 percent of all claims come tainted with fraud. They simply figure it into their rates.

Taking something directly from someone looks and feels

wrong. Strange how taking through the system can look and feel shrewd.

Tony Mascari usually caddies for professional golfer Chi-Chi Rodriguez. Tony grew up in a tough neighborhood. During the 1973 Masters Golf Tournament, he confided to a reporter that, as a boy, he stood on the brink of "going bad." But his dad talked him out of it. Why?

"Dad told me," said Mascari, "'More money has been stolen by a smart man with an attaché case than a dumb man with a gun.'"

*U.S. News and World Report* for 12 March 1973, ran an article on "New Style in Public Enemies—The White-Collar Criminal." It began by telling how crime in the streets gets the headlines, but white-collar crime such as fraud, embezzlement, tax evasion, and bribery is costing this nation many times as much as the route taken by all the robbers, burglars, and muggers. Senator Allan Bible of Nevada, chairman of the Senate Select Committee on Small Business warns,

White-collar crime is the type of crime that can have a serious influence on the social fabric of the nation and is costing the American consumer millions of dollars in higher prices and lost tax revenue. . . . We have heard it said that a little man can steal a bottle of milk from the doorstep and he goes to jail in a hurry. But a business tycoon can steal thousands or millions of dollars and probably won't ever see the inside of a prison.

Or how about my support of social traditions that deny education or job opportunity to minority or poorer persons? Such attitudes practically insure them of a lifelong low income. Yet I don't feel particularly criminal or even sinful about supporting such traditions.

So, to understand when taking becomes stealing, I need some clarity on ownership. Suppose the earth is the Lord's and everything in it. Then private property is not a right. It's a trust. Things get terribly confused when men begin to argue that property is somehow a sacred right in which government and God must not meddle.

I remember playing mumbletypeg as a boy, with jackknives, out in our backyard. Two or three of us would get together. We'd mark out a square in the dirt. Then we would throw our jackknives, and depending on the angle of the throw, we'd divide up the property. As the game heated up, we'd get into arguments about what property belonged to whom. But, no matter how much we argued, or cut up the property, all of it still belonged to my father.

The words "You shall not steal" help me penetrate the kind of spiritual reality that will make material sense. I can't tell where my material body leaves off and my spirit begins. The way I relate to the material stuff of life directly affects my spiritual health. And vice versa.

What does it mean to me that "the earth is the Lord's?" It means I need to examine all human economic systems in the light of his declared ownership of everything. I need to judge economic theories in the light of God's declared intention that the earth and everything in it be used for the fulfillment of all life.

Such thoughts have some disturbing implications to me as an American. The world I live in has material limits. Such a world literally will not let all people live as most Americans now live, surrounded by automobiles, television, and central heating. Furthermore, rich countries keep getting richer and poor countries poorer. Suddenly I begin to sense why leaders of small countries so often sound angry and resentful.

Dr. Donald W. Shriver, in an essay, "Cardiff: Repentance and our Survival," which appeared in the *Presbyterian Outlook* makes some arresting observations. For two hundred years Western countries have used natural resources from all over the world to support their standard of living. Our country alone today uses 40 percent of the world's annual output of natural resources to support its 6 percent of the world's population. Since World War II the poorer countries have heard us say that if they work hard they can develop too.

But now Western ecologists tell them, "Sorry, it turns out that too much industrial wealth will destroy the earth's environment. Besides we have a far more limited supply of resources than we once thought. So you better give up your dreams of becoming as rich as we are."

Such advice sounds evil enough to make whole countries fighting mad. Who gave the countries north of the equator the right to use the lion's share of the world's fuel, metal, and clean air? It should not surprise me to hear people in developing countries say: "Who are you to tell us we have to limit our growth in the name of 'ecology'? Forget it. We want our rights to pollute and our right to a larger share of the world's limited resources. If some one has to limit his growth let the rich countries limit theirs. In the name of justice let them cut back their economic consumption. We're tired of a world where some men have two cars and others do not even have two meals."

So, as my understanding of ownership deepens, I begin to see more clearly what stealing means. A man's life does not consist of the things he possesses. There's more to acquisition than simply taking. Do I take more than I need, simply to increase my status? If so, I may soon discover my possessions possessing me.

How many possessions are enough? If I have two pairs of shoes, will twelve make me happier? Slowly, I begin to see through advertising that urges me to discover "wants" I can only fulfill with surplus money and a credit card.

I might rediscover my soul if I lowered my standards of living. A man can smother his soul under a pile of possessions.

Not that I think Jesus put a premium on poverty. Men need the good things of earth to support their lives. Wealthy nations must take the first steps in providing basic materials for their poorest citizens. Why can't we use economic growth as a support system to enrich the spirit of man as well as his socioeconomic system?

Neither rich nor poor live by bread alone. Yet the potential for spiritual growth of either needs material support.

Stealing means taking hold of the good stuff of this world and claiming it as my own to do with as I please, irrespective of the needs of my brother.

Yet such people soon feel trapped in an unfeeling universe

where no one cares for them. They create a world where each must fend for himself the best he can.

Isn't that the deepest theft of all? The idea that we belong to no one but ourselves? That we are strictly on our own? Again I stand in the shadow of the Cross. God meets me there. He doesn't have to say much. Suddenly I see. He paid a great price for me. I can't begin to measure my own value. All men mean that much to God.

God gave himself. That's the secret. That kind of giving frees men to live. And God nourishes my spirit as I give. If I give a cup of cold water, a pair of shoes, a ten-dollar bill, God has a chance to enlarge my soul. Life is not simply for the taking, but for the giving. If that's true, then it is better to give than to receive.

I begin by giving myself to him who gave himself for me.

From there, I can go on to give myself to people nearest to me. I can begin by giving them time, and attention, and understanding.

From there I can begin to reexamine the priorities of my life. What criteria will I use in the management of what I have? I can begin to make such judgments out of concern for the good they will produce instead of what profit they will bring. That helps keep me from trying to squeeze more out of this world than there is in it. I'm free to open the doors of life to those who find such doors shut against them because of poverty, or hunger, or other aching human needs.

We may yet have time to develop economic systems that will help our society contribute to the physical and spiritual health of its people. What system is any good that fails to pass such a test?

Years ago, the city of Toledo had a mayor called "Golden Rule Jones." Once in a while, he went down to preside at police court. On a winter day, during the depression of the 1930s, the police brought in a man charged with stealing groceries. The man pleaded guilty, and offered no excuse except that he had no money and no job.

"I've got to fine you," said the mayor. "You stole, not from the community responsible for these conditions, but from a

particular man. So I fine you ten dollars." But then the mayor
reached into his pocket, pulled out a bill, and said, "Here's
the money to pay your fine." Then he picked up his hat and
handed it to the bailiff. "Now I'm going to fine everybody
in this courtroom fifty cents or as much thereof as he happens
to have with him, for living in a town where a man has to
steal groceries in order to eat. Bailiff, go through the courtroom and collect the fines and give them to the defendant."

So I have the economic responsibility not simply for my
family, but for the weakest member of my human race. "To
whom much is given, much will be required."

## QUESTIONS FOR REFLECTION AND DISCUSSION

1. What reasons do people give in attempting to justify stealing?
   Do you think any of the reasons are valid?
2. Do you see private property as a right or a trust? Why? Why not?
3. What other situations, beside outright theft, might be covered
   by this commandment?
4. How much do you need to be satisfied and happy?
5. In what sense, if any, do you think economic problems are also
   spiritual problems?

# 9. COMMUNICATION AND TRUTH

> You shall not bear false witness against your neighbor.
> *Exodus 20:16*

Why don't we understand each other? Why does lack of communication disrupt so much of personal and national life?

A reporter sat in jail. Why? Because he refused to tell the sources of his news story. The judge held him in contempt of court. But if the reporter revealed his sources, he would destroy his lines of communication. Who in the future would feel free to come forward with information critical of those in authority?

Centuries ago in Rome, a handful of men made decisions affecting the lives of millions. They felt the less people knew about national and international affairs, the better the government got along.

Free men, on the other hand, require open lines of communication to intelligently shape their lives and their society.

Yet communication remains one of the most troubled areas of personal and public life. Communication breaks down between all kinds of people. We talk together about the same thing, but fail to understand each other. A man and woman meet at a party and begin talking about happiness. Happiness to the man means having everything he wants in a world of his own. He happens to want a woman. However, he already has a wife. In fact, he has had her for a long time. So, in order to have the woman that he wants, he has to divorce his wife and leave his family.

The woman talking with him meant something entirely different by happiness. Happiness to the man meant having everything he wanted. To the woman happiness meant being everything she could be.

So, as they talked, the man said, "I have a right to be happy." The woman replied, "You have a responsibility to be good." Neither one understood the other.

Communication never has and never will be easy. Even Jesus couldn't always communicate with the men closest to him.

Communication depends upon a common understanding of and respect for truth. Truth makes communication happen. Sometimes without words, sometimes in spite of words. Sounds easy. Until I think about it a little.

"You shall not bear false witness against your neighbor." Like most people I make an effort to tell the truth. I try not to let circumstances, however embarrassing, push me into a lie. Yet the tone of my voice can give the lie to the words coming out of my mouth. The tone tells how I really feel about what I'm saying. And that feeling comes across far stronger than the words themselves. The tone of my voice when I say "I love you" to my wife betrays the truth of what I really feel about the information the words contain.

Yet words remain powerful symbols. It's just that the way I understand everything continues to change. That's not surprising. As a six-year-old, I saw and thought of my mother in a particular way. I described her in terms of what I thought and saw. But I don't describe her that way today. In a sense, she's the same person. But my understanding of her and my love for her has extended and deepened.

I find that happening in just about every area of life. I have to change the words I use, because words have a way of getting out of date. Besides, I know my words will never paint the picture for others that I want them to see. I simply have trouble telling the truth.

Josh Billings once commented: "As scarce as truth is, the supply has always been in excess of the demand." Still, unless

we try to get at this essential base to communications, sus-
picion and distrust develop. We feel we're speaking in different tongues, even when we're all speaking English.

Now God has a stake in all this. A great stake. When communication between people breaks down, God loses one of
his best ways of relating to us. I believe we have a religion of
incarnation. God comes to me in the flesh. God revealed
himself, his nature, his purpose, in the flesh of his prophets,
and finally in his Son.

Everything I know of this God suggests that he has strong
feelings about the free flow of information. He goes to great
lengths to let people know his plans. I get the picture of God
going out of his way to establish direct personal communication with each one of us.

Because God cares about communication he said, "You
shall not bear false witness against your neighbor." The
word "witness" reminds me of a couple of times I've had to
testify in court. And then my mind goes back to another
trial. The accused stands facing the judge, who stares mood-
ily back at him. The charge calls for the death sentence. But
there's no jury. An odd trial. All the evidence goes against
the defendant, but nobody in the courtroom believes him
guilty.

The judge breaks a brief silence to ask, "Tell me, what have
you done?" I wonder what went through the mind of Jesus
when Pilate asked that question. What had he done? Three
brief years. What had he done? At the start, he told the
messengers of John the Baptizer, "The blind receive their
sight and the lame walk, lepers are cleansed and the deaf
hear, and the dead are raised up, and the poor have good
news preached to them." What had he done? He had sown
a seed and he believed that seed had taken root in the hearts
of eleven men.

But none of that would interest Pilate. Jesus and everyone
else in the room knew he would not get out of this alive.
Events now swept him toward their climax. The judge went
out to the crowd. They demanded death. Pilate tried to wash
his hands of the whole thing. The crowd, in a burst of truth

greater than they knew, cried, "His blood be on us and on our children!"

In that confused and contradictory setting, Jesus said something someone remembered. "For this I was born, and for this I have come into the world, to bear witness to the truth."

"Truth? What is truth?" asks Pilate. He saw so little of it in his world. Does truth exist? How many have asked that question? Not in cynical disbelief, but in desperate need. We ask it often in secret, painful silence. Parents, as they look at the picture of a son killed in Southeast Asia. Others as they read in the newspapers about duplicity in high places.

No wonder a large number of students claim they see nothing wrong with cheating on tests at school. Many students claim they simply reflect the attitudes of the world of adults. One survey says that only 2 percent of college students think "courage to stand up for your ideas" pays off in business. Aggressiveness is the characteristic they believe most important (59 percent voting for it), with intelligence and "playing the angles," the next two qualities regarded as profitable in the adult world, as they see it.[1]

Subtly, society conditions me to think things will fall apart if I tell the truth. Yes, I want my children to tell the truth, the whole truth, and nothing but the truth—until we have guests in the house.

What about truth in advertising? I read the new car ads. The cars sound sophisticated, luxurious, and sexually appealing. I read the ad and pick up the impression that if I buy this car, with it comes a magical personal transformation. The car is secondary. Too often, it is designed to fall apart in three or four years anyway. But the ad implies it will benefit me spiritually. So it becomes a kind of icon.

No wonder Pilate asked, "What is the truth?" And without waiting for an answer, he left the room. Like me, he had seen manipulators of public opinion, interested in their success rather than the truth. People who to get my vote or my bus-

1. William M. Ramsay, "In Response to God," *Presbyterian Outlook*, 3 November 1969, p. 13.

iness, will select little parts of the truth which will lead me to a certain conclusion. They will tell me true facts but leave me with a false impression. Manipulation of an idea becomes more important than the integrity of an idea.

And suddenly I see that truth comes in bigger packages than simply statements that agree with facts. Truth comes in meanings that match reality. That's the essence of it.

I've seen people use facts as the enemy of truth. A man could say, "I saw Art Sueltz walking down Fifth Avenue in April with a blonde." That statement agrees with the facts, but it could leave a false impression, unless the speaker also went on to say, "The blonde was his wife."

In 1969, several thousand young people gathered in Griffith Park, Los Angeles. The following Monday morning, a story appeared in the Los Angeles *Times*. It began like this, "An estimated 12,000 hippies did their own thing in Griffith Park's merry-go-round area Sunday, celebrating something called 'park-in' with confusion, toplessness and one case of complete nudity . . ." Now all three statements agree with the facts. But if, like me, you read the first paragraph and then go on to something else, you could infer meanings from the facts that do not match the realities. Farther down the column, in the third paragraph, the article goes on to say: "The crowd was orderly and law-abiding, even the nudist, who was only three years old, and the topless ones were mostly, if not entirely, male." [2]

Now that kind of trifling with truth uses statements that agree with facts to communicate meanings about other people that do not check out with reality. And that's what it means to "bear false witness."

No wonder Pilate asked, "What is truth?" Suddenly I see that truth goes beyond a bare statement of fact. Truth means conveying true impressions. That affects my use of the facts. I sense myself entering a whole new dimension of reality.

Centuries ago, Greek architects discovered that if you carve a column absolutely straight, it will give the impression of

2. *Los Angeles Times*, 22 September 1969, p. 1.

curving in on itself. If you want a column to look straight, it could not be straight. You have to make it swell in the middle and taper at the ends. So the Greeks carved their columns that way.

Furthermore, the axis of the columns in a well-designed temple inclined slightly inward, so that when you look at them, they appear straight up and down. If you put them straight up and down, it would look as if the columns splayed out.

This architectural distortion of straightness in order to give the appearance of straightness tells me something about the truth. It does not make truth an entirely subjective affair, as Pilate suspected. It does not mean I can say anything that seems expedient. It does mean that if a man pounds on my study door waving a gun and saying he's going to shoot his wife the minute he finds her, I will not tell him that she left just three minutes ago.

Communicating truth presupposes a congruence between what I say and the essence of my life. How I say what I say, in a curious way, reveals who I am. Such words become an extension of my being. If truth exists, it exists in persons. If absolute truth exists, and the New Testament keeps insisting that it does, then it exists in an absolute person. Apart from that, we're adrift in the shallow waters of expedience and duplicity.

The men of the New Testament keep saying such absolute truth exists. And they go on to say, "The word became flesh and dwelt among us, full of grace and truth."

They say that truth comes close to us in Jesus Christ. I receive personal truth not so much by observation as by revelation. To know the truth about French or physics usually means reading books and memorizing facts and performing experiments. I try to get something into my head. But such facts often have little to do with my personal values or behavior.

When Jesus said, "I came to bear witness to the truth," he was talking about the kind of truth that gives shape and integrity to human life and society. Honesty means more than frankness. It has to do with relationships. Knowing the truth happens in the context of a relationship.

I begin to know the truth as I trust Jesus enough to follow him. In that relationship, I begin to know the truth that sets me free to be human. The kind of truth that puts me in my right mind. Opens my eyes. Rouses my slumbering spirit, so that hope begins to grow where despair had frosted the ground. Such truth helps me rise above a thousand kinds of slavery, to become the kind of person Art Sueltz was meant to be. Freedom to face the truth about myself and still believe I am exactly the kind of person loved by God. Accepted by him. Forgiven by him, and restored to a place of dignity and honor in his family. That's the truth I need to know.

That kind of truth sets me free not only to accept myself, but sets me free to love and trust my brother. And I believe that is the basic truth upon which communication can begin to take place. I need to send my roots into that spiritual reality.

Suddenly I'm free to reexamine cherished opinions I have used to support my sensitive ego for so long. I can begin tearing down some of my defenses that make learning from others so terribly hard.

"For this cause, I came into the world," said Jesus, "and for this reason I was born, that I might bear witness to the truth. . . . If you continue in my word, you are truly my disciples, and you will know the truth, and the truth will make you free."

If we really have an incarnational religion, then knowing the truth has a further horizontal dimension. I mean, I know the truth about myself as I reveal myself to another person. That takes courage. Jesus was never too proud to do that. He was never too proud to say what he felt and believed. Even when it upset his plans. He was never too proud to accept the authority of truth and love. He was never afraid to tell someone else how he believed that person should act in a given situation.

All of this makes truth hard to give and hard to take. How

many refuse to accept any authority except the authority of their own conscience? And sometimes for good reasons. But others refuse to accept truth for bad reasons or for no reason at all.

On the other hand, how many of us fear revealing the truth that we have received? How many parents live in fear of telling their children what is right and wrong? They fear repressing their children and making them psychopathic adults. Or perhaps they don't want to make their children look odd among their own friends.

I have to ask myself as a minister of the Gospel, "Am I, for one reason or another, afraid to say, 'This is the Gospel. This we know about God as we have seen him in Christ. We welcome questions and critical interest. Sure, sometimes we get on the wrong track, but this we believe, here we stand'?"

In an advertisement for *Psychology Today*, the editors quote Marvin Franel in an article "Morality in Psychotherapy." The year, 1930; the place, Berlin.

You are a practicing psychoanalyst confronting an interesting new patient. His name is Adolf Hitler; he is a practicing politician, regarded as one of the country's rising young men. Now he has come to you because he is troubled by persistent anxieties. He speaks confidently about his plans for Germany, yet he admits to fear of failure, and therefore punishment by "lesser beings." Lately, however, when he considers some of the harsh deeds demanded by his grandiose plans, he has been bothered by feelings of guilt. Nevertheless, he is convinced that the ends justify the means. He is bothered only because his increasing anxieties and guilt feelings may impede him in the execution of his designs. Hitler asks you to put an end to these disturbing feelings. Can you help him?

In that circumstance would I have the courage of my convictions?

The early Christians felt considerable tension between themselves and their society. They had determined to make clear the judgment of God on the world's values. Obeying God rather than men, they never expected everybody to speak well of them.

Yet that tension had a redemptive quality. These men did not set out to make themselves unpopular irritants in society. They hoped God would use them to change men and institutions. Because they refused to conform to the way things went in the world, the world began to change.

In that sense, Christians lived as a subversive community, letting loose the truth and having as their goal the will of God on earth as in heaven.

So Jesus reminds me that the truth has an authority all its own. That's a fact of creation. And a mature person learns how to handle it. He learns how to respond to the truth and how to live by it. At a critical point in someone else's life I may speak for God. That could be the most important thing I do on earth. If God speaks to me through other people, who am I to presume he will not speak to others through me?

Communicating truth will always seem irrelevant to many things people want most. People want freedom. The truth is, the only freedom we ever get is the freedom of being bound to something. People want money and the things money buys. The truth is, if I give money away, seek first the really valuable things, the things of God's kingdom, I can then let the other things come in due time. People want escape from pain and trouble. The truth is, I have my own cross to bear.

So in one sense, truth always seems irrelevant to the immediate concerns of human beings.

Yet, it remains crucial to everything we do. Death and meaninglessness stare us in the face. But we have seen the death of Jesus on the Cross. We have seen life rise out of that death. Because of these two things, nothing remains totally meaningless and beyond the reach of love. That prepares me to tackle the problems of life. Public or private.

The world doesn't wait eagerly for our Christian message. The world couldn't care less if that truth ever gets preached. Still, I can use every means at hand to demonstrate that the truth of our Gospel is indispensable—that it addresses the issues of our time.

## QUESTIONS FOR REFLECTION AND DISCUSSION

1. Do you think it's ever OK to tell a lie? Why? Why not?
2. Have you ever found communication breaking down between those closest to you? When?
3. In what sense or in what circumstances do you have trouble telling the truth? Why?
4. Should advertisers be held accountable for the truth of their claims?
5. Is it easier to judge a political candidate's truthfulness by watching him or her on television, or in person?

# 10. WHAT DO WE WANT?

> You shall not covet your neighbor's house; you shall not
> covet your neighbor's wife, or his manservant, or his maid-
> servant, or his ox, or his ass, or anything that is your
> neighbor's.
>
> *Exodus 20:17*

A neighbor once spotted Abraham Lincoln trying to separate
two of his sons, locked in a bloody-nosed battle. "What's the
matter, Mr. Lincoln?"

"Just what's the matter with the whole world," he answered. "I've got three walnuts and each boy wants two."

As a warning that my wants may make shipwreck of my
life, I hear, "Art, ye shall not covet your neighbor's house, nor
his wife . . . nor anything that is your neighbor's."

"Covet" means to want. What do I want? How much?
What will I do to get it? And by what criteria will I say
I have arrived and have what I want?

Suddenly I'm in new moral territory. The four preceding
commandments ask me to watch what I do. This one asks me
to watch what goes on in my heart. That's where coveting
takes place.

Harvey Cox in *Christianity and Crisis* commented on "The
Child Who Had to Have Things."

There once was a family that seemed to be pretty well fixed. Each
member had sufficient food, clothing, education, and leisure time.
Even their radio was, for its time, a marvel of efficiency. But one
day the son came home from school saying "Somebody has invented
a radio that shows pictures. We simply must have one." And lo, in
the light of such heartfelt necessity, a television set was purchased.

A few years later the same son came home from high school saying, "Somebody has just invented a television set that shows pictures in color. We simply must have one." And lo, in the light of such heartful necessity, a color TV set was purchased.

A few years later still the same son came home from college saying, "Somebody has just invented a rotary engine that is quieter and more efficient than the old piston jobs. We simply must have one." And lo, in the light of such heartfelt necessity, a Mazda was purchased to replace the Ford.

Moral: Invention is the mother of necessity.

I grew up encouraged to succeed. I got that encouragement everywhere. I got it at home, at school, from athletic coaches. As a result, I often worked for better grades in school, rather than for a real understanding of the subject.

Yet I believe in excellence. Doing a job well. It can produce satisfaction.

I remember the man who coached us at the University of California. When I rowed on the university crew, he would get us together in the locker room before a race. One particular day, before we rowed Washington for the West Coast championship, he reminded us of the motto over the Olympic Stadium, "It's not whether you win or lose, but how you play the game." "That's a nice sentiment, boys," commented the coach, "but you guys better win!"

I wondered afterward if he really meant that winning is more important than anything else. Dimly, it dawned on me that wanting to win can easily turn into an attitude that assumes anything goes, so long as you succeed. I'm beginning to see what can happen in a world where simply winning elections determines morals and values. How it twists people, communities, and institutions. Wanting to win can suddenly become lust for power and set a nation against itself.

Furthermore, my wants can keep me from accepting myself. I can begin to make grim comparisons of myself with somebody else. For instance, I begin looking at someone else who already has what I want. He has arrived where I want to get. How I torture myself, knowing that he is or has, what I hope to be or want to get.

In the heat of such feelings, I seldom stop to ask whether his goals ought to be my goals. Would his goals really satisfy me? Why do I think that if I could be as strong, or as talented, or as handsome, or as intelligent, or as confident, as somebody else, I would feel satisfied with myself? What makes me so sure I'd be happier than somebody else? So my wants subtly lead me to doubt God's wisdom in making me as I am.

As a result, I chronically want more than I have. Like a lot of other people, I feel underprivileged in my own eyes. In the Middle Ages, men thought it a virtue to go without things. Today, such an attitude feels like sin. Dr. G. R. Davies, in *The Sin of Our Age*, commented that the good life has become inseparable from the maximum possible consumption of things. This new religion stresses the increasing of wants, as though happiness and satisfaction in life come from an insatiable appetite. "As a result men are no longer judged poor by what they consume, but by what they think they should consume."

Somehow, society says to me that a man who wants a lot of things is a good man. As though a rich man is a good man and a poor man is a bad man. It further assumes that a man who has a lot of money also has good ideas about education, politics, morality, and religion. Strange how a rich man's ideas carry weight all out of proportion to their intrinsic value.

I believe God made a good world. He put good things in it. He built me so I'd want these good things. So how much territory is covered by the warning, "Art, you shall not covet"? What constitutes a life-disrupting desire for the good things of life?

I feel that piling up things beyond what I need seriously endangers my human spirit. Men and their societies get in trouble when they want more than they can possibly use. Then wants become "dogs in the manger." A dog doesn't eat hay or oats or corn. He can't use them. But he can sit in the manger and bark and snap. He can snarl at hungry horses and hungry cattle and prevent their eating. My wants become covetous when I want what I cannot possibly use and am unwilling to let others make use of.

How that spirit destroys and disrupts a human family!

Often, the best-selling novels lie to us. They tell me that a man and woman passionately in love (therefore, ideally suited), can't help but make a go of the marriage. They ask me to believe that passionate emotional attachment will overcome innate selfishness and make people forebearing, sacrificial, and considerate. They ask me to believe that by some magic, a willful, pleasure-loving young woman and a willful, pleasure-loving young man, because of their fascination for each other, will somehow adjust to each other's tastes and competing desires, in a world of selfishness.

I've seen people get married on that basis. Both want what they want. Both want luxury. Both want the whole world for themselves. And before long, they want out of a relationship that puts an intolerable strain on both of them.

Now, such unchecked desire creates real hazards on a broader scale. Barbara Ward, in her compelling fashion, comments on the theory of "trickle-down" economic assistance. She mentions how the president of the World Bank pointed out in a recent speech that some countries, among them Brazil and Mexico, have grown overall by 6 or 7 percent in the last ten years. But, while that has happened, the share of the richest 10 percent has grown by at least 10 percent—to well over a third of the wealth in the country —while the share of the poorest 40 percent has actually fallen by 10 percent. The rich have gotten richer, and the poor have gotten poorer.

Besides that maldistribution, there is another difficulty. If the poor of all the world can be fed and clothed and housed only after an enormous expansion of wealth and consumption has taken place, in the Western world, those poorer areas may find that there are not enough resources to go around. For instance, if every country wanted to imitate America in passenger cars—God forbid—we would have at least three and one-half billion cars on this planet by 1990. Imagine what that would do to gasoline supplies. Imagine how it would heat up

the atmosphere. And suppose, at the same time, every person
in the world had at his or her disposal America's present supply
of power per head. That is, the equivalent of thirteen metric
tons of coal per year. What would that do to the energy
reserves of the world?

I remember a story Jesus told. A story about a man to
whom God said, "You fool. You poor fool . . ." The story
of a small barn and a big fool. In the story, a man worked
hard and planned thoroughly and got what he wanted. A
self-made man. Jesus didn't condemn him for that. His success remained neutral. You can't praise or blame him until
you ask, "How did he get that way?" And more importantly,
"What will he do now that he has arrived?" That's what
worried Jesus every time he saw a successful man.

One day this man goes out to take an inventory of his
siloes, granaries, barns, and finds them too small. He can't
let his crop rot in the field. On the basis of his findings, he
decides to tear down his warehouses and build bigger ones.
Jesus finds nothing wrong with that. The test comes later.

After giving the order to build the siloes and barns, the
man goes out to inspect the progress. And Jesus lets us read
his mind as the man walks through the construction area.
We hear him saying to himself, "This is it. You've made it.
After a slow start, after all those years of hard work, all
those years of planning, you've arrived. Look at it. Security
that will help you laugh at the years. You can relax and
take it easy. You've got it made."

And then Christ asks me to listen for a kind of rustling,
as though someone standing by listening suddenly decided
to leave. So I listen for a voice that speaks quietly in passing,
like a breeze that blows across the field. Not a gentle voice,
and yet more impatient than severe. As if God, for all his
disappointment, still cared deeply about this man. "You fool,
you poor fool. You feel so secure with your little farm. At
sundown, I'm calling you to me for an accounting. Where will
your resources, your security be then?"

Now when someone calls me a sinner, that's one thing. I

may even feel flattered. But when someone calls me a fool, that gets under my skin. But Jesus risks my anger to warn me I can repeat the mistake of the man who simply wanted bigger barns. A hard-working man, a decent man, an honest man, but a man who thought he could satisfy his wants by a barnful of this or that.

And suddenly, it dawns on me. It's not an issue of whether I'm going to be good or bad or selfish or generous. The question is whether or not I'm going to let the good things of this world make a fool of me. As a warning, I hear, "Art, you shall not covet. You shall not covet what somebody else is, or what he has. If you do, you will miss the joy of being who you are and having what you have."

I need a deep healing of my wants. The kind of healing that will contribute to the fulfillment of my person, so I can contribute to the fulfillment of the life of other persons.

How does such healing come? Do you remember the first time you fell in love? Perhaps as a freshman in high school? How did you get over it? How did you forget that first boy or that first girl? If you're anything like me, you didn't get over it by taking those emotions out in the backyard and choking them to death. I got over them by falling in love with someone else.

And Jesus tells me to look for the healing of my wants in much the same way. If I want to get over the dissatisfaction my desires and wants can create within me, he says I ought to "seek first the kingdom of God and his righteousness, and then all these other things will be yours as well."

The inner release that I long for comes by way of a new affection. Such an openness to God enables him to free me to make the kinds of choices that will enlarge my life and the lives of other men.

The freedom to accept and like myself, without forever wanting to be someone else. A freedom to enjoy what I have, without forever feeling driven to want what I do not have. And, for his part, God promises to provide me with all I need to make me happy to be myself. Then I can creatively contribute to meeting my neighbor's needs. Then I can genuinely feel happy for his achievement and truly pleased by his good fortune.

The New Testament reminds me that shattering changes took place in the disciples' way of doing things. But their sense of God's continual presence in each moment of their lives gave them marvelous resilience. They grew up learning to say their prayers in the temple. But driven out of there they began to worship in private homes. They constantly shifted their strategy as God gave them the future and it became their present moment.

Now I'm old enough and human enough to dislike abrupt, swift changes. But I also believe that the men who wrote the Old and New Testaments made no mistake when they tell me that I'm better off to greet the future with open arms as it comes to meet me than in trying to resist it. God comes to meet me in the future.

This rediscovery of God's presence in every moment of time and beyond has a way of pulling things together for me. It's like the center of a circle that gives all the points on the circumference their meaning. Without such a center the future as well as the present seems chaotic and life feels out of control. Issues about the dignity of people, respect for women, care of bodies and souls, concern for children, peace, liberation, brotherhood, economics, political action, all have meaning and significance in relation to God's presence in Christ at the center of each moment. Cut that heart out and life gets perverted.

Long ago, Moses came to the end of his leadership and had to stay in the desert as his people went over the Jordan River into the land of promise. The people faced an unknown and uncertain future. Moses worried about them. These people had put their pasts behind them. In unforgettable, urgent words, Moses appealed to them, "Choose life and then you and your descendants will live. Love the Lord your God, obey and hold fast to him. That is life for you . . ."

Dr. Ernest Gordon, dean of the chapel at Princeton University, recalled not long ago that when Hitler rose to power and the Nazis darkened the land with their great shadow, the members of the German Confessing Church recognized that the call to choose life had to be heard and honored in their country regardless of what it cost. So they met to interpret their faith in a document we now call "The Theological Declaration of Barmen." In it they said, "We reject the false doctrine, as though there were areas of our life in which we belong not to Jesus Christ, but to other lords—areas in which we could not need justification and sanctification through him."

Such words remind me of Christ's presence and authority in every moment and over all life. I suddenly see his presence as a threat to anyone else who would try to control my mind or my heart at any time in any way. Yes, I think I do see huge threatening shadows looming around me in the present and in the future. Yet I also sense that though God has given me no blueprint for tomorrow, he has given me the assurance that there will be a tomorrow. A tomorrow worthy of him and his gospel.

In this time of unprecedented strain, I still hear a voice that sounds down through the ages, "Fear not . . . it is your Father's good pleasure to give you the kingdom." And I see my response to that voice in what the New Testament calls repentance. That is, turning from despair to hope—from death to life. Why be afraid of life, now or ever?

## QUESTIONS FOR REFLECTION AND DISCUSSION

1. How do you feel about this statement: "Invention is the mother of necessity"?
2. Have you ever wished you were somebody else? Why? Why not?
3. What will it take to make you happy?
4. What are your expectations for the future? How closely are your hopes tied to your material prosperity?
5. Do you feel pressures in your neighborhood or at your job to "keep up with the Joneses"? Are those pressures good or bad? How can they be resisted?